Living in the shadow of tyranny
How I deceived the Nazis to survive the war

- The Isaac Kraicer story -

As told to S.J. Helgesen

Copyright © 2018
S.J. Helgesen

Dedication

I have touched and been touched by many souls who have protected and loved me during my life. Without their kindness and selflessness, I would not be here today to tell my story. It is to them I dedicate this book. To my beloved family from Gostynin and Zychlin who nurtured me, encouraged me and showed me that life has no guarantees, but plenty of opportunities; to those who didn't know my secret identity but who managed to change their minds about people they didn't know; and to my dear wife, Rachel, my sons, John and Leonard and my daughter, Zahava and all their children and our two great grandchildren. I thank them for validating my existence by being the loving people they are. I ask the Almighty to bless them and show them the path to all their hopes and dreams.

Acknowledgements

I am pleased to acknowledge the efforts of a man I have come to know and admire and one who I am proud to call my friend, the 'teller of my tale,' Stephan Helgesen. Like the ship that took me to my new home in Israel after the Holocaust, 'Providence,' he has helped me carry my story across the oceans of the literary world so that it might be shared with everyone. Providence has brought those of us who experienced and survived the darkness of unimaginable years of tyranny to the bright light of day where there are no shadows for evil to hide. Finally, I acknowledge the power of faith, hope, determination and forgiveness. Were it not for these, none of us would have a place in the sun.

Introduction

Every life is remarkable. Each one honors the Creator with its own individual potential to rise from innocent beginnings and enrich the rest of humanity with its actions. Each life contributes a splash of color to the eternal tapestry of mankind, but more importantly, it offers a place to anchor another new life's knot to those already there. By connecting ourselves, we all accept our unique role in humanity's grand design.

We find our meaning from many sources. History gives us a larger context, a backdrop, in front of which we gradually place our own wisdom, gleaned from personal experiences and from our time spent with people we have come to know, love and respect. Each person adds to our lives, sometimes in mysterious ways, sometimes in obvious ones. The average human being will meet or be exposed to thousands of people in a lifetime, and we must never minimize nor ignore the many chance encounters that life offers us...for we never know just exactly where they will take us. Such was my special encounter with Isaac Kraicer.

Isaac was introduced to me by his brother-in-law, Aron Straser. Aron sent me Isaac's memoirs about his teenage years in occupied Poland. Aron was another Polish Holocaust survivor whose story I had the privilege of telling in 2013 ("My Name is Aron: Journey to the light of freedom"). He died in May of this year, may God rest his soul, but his spirit and memory will always be with me and with the many people he touched in his 92 years. Isaac's wife, Rachel, is Aron's twin sister from Smorgon, Poland, and she and Isaac have been married since 1947 after meeting one another in the Nazi concentration camp, Bergen-Belsen, after the war. Theirs is an inspiring story of hope, love and devotion.

While writing this book about Isaac I was struck by the absolute polar opposite childhoods he and I had, separated by more than two decades and by thousands of miles. When Isaac was running _for_ his life, I was running _alongside_ mine.

When he lived in constant fear of being discovered a Jew, I enjoyed the acceptance of my family for just being me. It is no wonder that given the atrocities that many survivors endured (not the least of which was having their entire families wiped out) many of them have never been able to live what the rest of us would consider _normal_, post-Holocaust lives. Those that have been able to deal with their adversity are testimony to the kind of courage and determination that often resides in those who have suffered abuse at the hands of others.

Holocaust survivors are unique in the type of emotional and mental distress they bear. _The closest we can come in our day is servicemen returning home after years of battle._ Nightmares continue to haunt them and daytime realities often exchange places with events that occurred years earlier. I have great respect for those that have conquered their past but also great empathy with those who haven't.

Telling Isaac Kraicer's story has been more than a privilege for me. It has helped me affix my own knot in the tapestry of life that includes the Jews' survival in the Shoah. Most of all, I have gained a new friend in the bargain. Shalom, shalom.

Contents

Chapter I
My homeland

I suspect that my entrance into the world on May 22, 1925 in Gostynin, Poland was uneventful to the rest of my village but not to my parents, grandparents, uncles and aunts, of course. My birth name was Isaac Nachum Krajcer but my parents called me, Yitzak. (I changed the spelling of my family's name to the more easily pronounceable, Kraicer when I emigrated to the United States.) Winter was officially over two months earlier and Spring had begun. It was a good time to be born. These were the 'interwar years.' The wildflowers were responding to the relatively mild daytime temperatures though the nights were still somewhat chilly I am told. Weather controlled much of our lives then as it still does today.

The 'Great War' had gone on for years before Poland gained its independence. In 1916, the German and Austrian emperors attempted to increase Polish support for the Central Powers and to raise a Polish army so they declared that a new state called the Kingdom of Poland would be created and a puppet-like government was established in November of 1917.

My homeland was split during the partitions between Austria-Hungary and the German and Russian empires. Russia defended Serbia and was an ally of Britain and France against leading members of the Central Powers, Germany and Austria-Hungary. I would, of course, not know any of this until many years later when I studied the history of my country in school. As a small boy, I loved hearing about times past, especially those that had anything to do with my country. History was not uninteresting to me. It lived, and nothing that came before me was ever stale or boring.

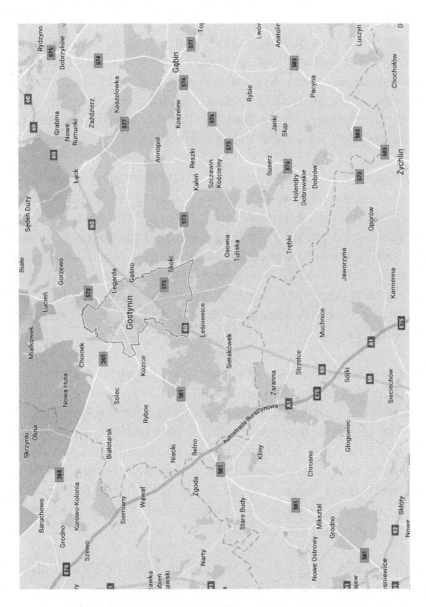

Map of Poland showing Gostynin and Zychlin

The First World War really set the tone for the two decades that followed. Two million Poles fought with the armies of the three occupying powers in WWI and just under a half-million were killed with about a million wounded. Hundreds of thousands of Polish civilians were moved to labor camps in Germany. The prevailing feeling was that both the Russians and the Germans were bad for Poland, but the edge (for badness) definitely went to the Germans.

The year 1917 was a pivotal year. The Americans had entered the war and the Russians were having to cope with a revolution which eventually took them off the eastern front. It also forced them to capitulate and sign the treaty of Brest-Litovsk in which Russia ceded all the former Polish land to the Central Powers of Germany and Austria-Hungary. THAT was something less than advantageous for us Poles, but the retreat of the Russians emboldened the Allies to press for Polish sovereignty.

The war was turning, and at this point I have to mention my parents' hero and the hero of all Polish Jews, General Jozef Pilsudski, a Polish patriot who was jailed for insubordination by the Germans towards the latter part of the war. Pilsudski was actually the 'guardian angel' of Poland and the Jews because of his steadfast defense of his country and his protectiveness towards those of my faith. In the Fall of 1918, the Hapsburg monarchy disintegrated and the imperial German government collapsed.

Pilsudski was released, and in November of 1918 he was given the reins of power by the Regency Council of the Kingdom of Poland, and he became the provisional Chief of State. For the first time in 123 years, Poland was reborn for all Poles of every ethnicity! That was the beginning of the end for domination of Poland...so my parents thought.

My father Eliezer and mother Golda Rivka

If I've learned one thing over the years, it's that history has a way of repeating itself, and that's why understanding context is important to fully understand people, their ideas, motivations and the decisions they take. Unfortunately, I've found that Americans of non-Polish descent know very little about Poland, nor do they know much about the First World War. I don't blame them. Except for a few souls, most people alive today were born after that terrible war. Poland has endured so much pain at the hands of occupiers and oppressors like the Russians and Germans, that it's no wonder that animosity for these two peoples still runs deep among my countrymen.

Pilsudski and Poland were a powerful combination, and my country was on an upward path towards prosperity, but danger was lurking - in Germany - in the shadows. When I was a boy of only eight or so, National Socialism hit the average German like a tidal wave. The Nazi Party was gaining strength and Adolf Hitler was sowing the seeds of Germany's return to the world stage as a superpower... and Poland was in his sights.

Before we relive that terrible time, let me bring you back to my little village of Gostynin, population approximately 4,000 at the time of the start of the war. Gostynin was the county seat and was founded in the 13th century. It is located on the Skrwa Lewa River, approximately 60 miles northwest of Warsaw and 14 miles southwest of the city of Plock. It is one of hundreds of smallish villages that dot the Polish landscape. There was no big industry, just farming, some lumbering, the fur business and some mercantile establishments. Most of the farms were about 5 kilometers from the town. There were three principal groups that made up the village: non-Jewish Polish-speaking Poles, non-Jewish German-speaking Poles and Polish and Yiddish-speaking Jews. The Jews numbered around 2,300.

They can trace their residency in Gostynin to about 1765, though there are reports that Jews owned a brewery and a malt factory there in 1626. In 1765, the community had about 157 members. Fourteen years later, a wooden synagogue was built near the marketplace, but it succumbed to a fire in 1899.

By the end of the 18th century, Jews comprised 26% of Gostynin's population. They were traders, innkeepers, butchers, tailors and furriers, and most of them lived in the center of town. The synagogue was located north of the marketplace, near where the train station is now situated.

By today's standards, the Gostynin of my youth was a pretty primitive place with dirt streets and no centralized water or sewage system. We had electricity, of course, but no indoor plumbing. We owned neither radio nor telephone - those were expensive luxury items.

Gostynin had the same shops and buildings that any small town would have, but in addition to those were two synagogues, a library with Jewish, Polish and German books, and a sports club. There were teachers that taught the Bible in the Hebrew language and a school for Orthodox girls.

We also had Zionist, Socialist, Orthodox parties and youth groups. I belonged to the Zionist group which I joined when I was eight or nine instead of the boy scouts which didn't take Jews. It seemed there was always some sort of festival happening, though most were Catholic. There was a cinema which was always a big attraction.

Gostynin town square in 1939

My earliest memories were of our family. We were a close-knit bunch with plenty of individual personalities to choose from. It's fair to say that my parents Eliezer, my father, and Golda Rivka (nee Korn) my mother were, you might say, traditional parents for their time: father was strict and mother was more lenient.

I loved them both, dearly, as I did my two brothers, Michal who was two years younger than me, born in 1927 and Szyja Faiwel who was the youngest of all of us, born in 1931. My paternal family was rather large and my grandfather was named Aron (my grandmother was deceased at the time of my birth). My maternal grandparents lived in the nearby village of Zychlin as did my uncles. We all spoke Yiddish at home and Polish when we were out among the villagers.

My father and his brothers (my uncles) and a brother-in-law were in business together. They bought local farmers' produce and livestock and sold all of it in Lodz and Warsaw. In those days, it took nearly four hours to get there. You would travel south to Kutno and then east to Warsaw (map). Mother would stay home with us.

My childhood was free-wheeling. I enjoyed my early school (a public Kindergarten) and later grade school, where all three ethnic groups attended. At school, they taught us Polish songs and dances in addition to the normal subjects. Sometimes I would get called a very unflattering name by other Polish boys. I asked my mother what this word, "Zyd" was and she said it wasn't nice at all. I remember many things from that time, like the huge sunflowers that dotted the area when our class went on 'field trips'.

I was a voracious reader. I read everything that I could get my hands on, although my mother was the *gatekeeper* on just what books I could take out from the library. I especially liked history. In history class, in school, I <u>became</u> all the great ancient figures (in my mind at least). I was a good student, but not the best. If you asked me what subject was my favorite, I would have to tell you that it was running!

I realize that running wasn't an actual subject, but running was an elixir to a small boy! I burned up energy, challenged myself and got rid of some of the tension of the day. Naturally, I loved soccer, but my parents didn't encourage it; they were afraid I would injure myself, but like many children, I respectfully ignored their warnings, but more on that in a bit.

School days weren't always without incident. One day, in seventh grade, when the teacher had his back turned to us, a boy sitting behind me (the son of a policeman) hit me hard and called me, "Zyd" a very nasty Polish word for Jew. I couldn't contain myself. I turned around and hit him and we began to fight. Every so often there would be altercations with Polish boys that were prejudiced against Jews.

I recall my brother, Michal, interfered in a fight when some Polish boys were beating up a red-haired boy. I was surprised when the very next day our Principal kissed Michal on the head! My religious education was rounded out by a Jewish teacher who came to our home to instruct me in the ways of the Jewish faith. He was a large man with a big beard from a fine family. I'm somewhat ashamed to say that it didn't take and my father told him after a few times that he should stop coming. I wasn't motivated; I admit it. I was never Bar Mitzvah'ed, but was nevertheless, a believer, so that seemed to satisfy my parents. I should mention that my mother was a student of history and would tell us stories about Jews through the ages that went all the way back to the Inquisition.

Everyone loved my mother, and she was a powerful influence in my life.

Back to running. I ran everywhere my legs could carry me (I had no bicycle). I ran to school, home from school and anywhere else I could, time permitting. There was a grove of beautiful Chestnut trees that begged to have a tyke like myself touch their branches as I ran through them. I remember one event that was kind of traumatic. I was playing a game of running in front of cars to see how close I could come to them without being hit, and my brother was playing, too. The car missed me and managed to graze my brother. That was the end of that game as mother laid down the law.

In Gostynin, I was known as the 'runner' by many people. Running was my way of connecting to the future. Let me explain. When you're walking, you're very much in the present, but when you're running, well, THEN you're touching the very nose of the future by your speed, leaving the present in the past! That was my belief, anyway. Running would later save my life, and I will tell you more about that later.

I would be remiss if I didn't say a word about food and romance. My mother was an excellent cook and creative, too. My mouth still waters when I think of her at the stove browning meat, making gravy, cooking sauerkraut and potatoes. The smells seemed to magically transform our little house into a palace of culinary pleasure. I was coming of age and was beginning to be interested in girls, but not in a very serious way. One Saturday I was walking home in the company of two girls who were really just good friends when I saw my parents across the street. I was a little embarrassed and left the girls and began walking towards my parents. When my mother saw this, she realized that I needed 'saving' so she said, "What are you doing Yitzak? Go back to the girls" which I immediately did.

It seems that my mother knew more about my situation than I did. By saying it was alright for me to walk with them she acknowledged my need for adolescent independence.

After suppers in my home there was time for the family to gather and read and talk before I was sent off to bed. I remember being afraid of the dark as a youngster. To cure me, my mother took me out into the backyard. She understood that I responded to logic, so she told me, "Yitzak, there is nothing here in the dark that isn't here in the light, so don't be afraid." It helped me conquer my fear.

As a small rural village, we were never far from meadows, forests, a river and farm animals of every sort. It was an idyllic place for a small boy. My friends and I explored every inch of town and the surrounding wooded area. The springs and summers were beautiful and the fall sobering (because it heralded the start of winter) and the winters, well, the winters were numbingly cold.

I relished each season and played every seasonal sport. My favorite sport was soccer as I mentioned (what else for a runner?), and I don't mind telling you that I was pretty good at it, too. They say that the best soccer players are those that live in the moment and like chess players are always thinking one or two moves ahead, always avoiding injuries but still taking chances. I definitely fell into that group as I managed to maneuver the ball around and avoided the many dangerous kicks to the shins from the opposing players.

In the winter, we would skate on the nearby ponds and lakes. Our 'skates' were usually nothing more than regular shoes, maybe with a little thin bark or some other material tied to them to improve their efficiency. Olympians we were not, but fun we did have.

Speaking of Olympians, my friends and I followed the 1936 Olympics in Berlin from the newspapers and newsreels. If you'll recall, that was the time when Hitler had polished up Berlin til it shined and placed great emphasis on his 'master race' winning in track. We all cheered when the black athlete, Jesse Owens, won the Gold Medal and beat out all of Hitler's Aryan runners!

One year's activities seemed to merge neatly into the next with no monumental changes until I became a teenager. It was then, in 1938, that we started hearing rumblings about growing nationalism in Germany. I wasn't concerned as the German-speaking Poles I knew weren't all that bad and nobody was talking about invasion or occupation or anything like that.

My parents knew better. They had lived through the First World War and knew that Germany had always had its eye on Poland and that one day our peace could be shattered. Tensions were rising. You could hear it in the adults' voices. Then, on September 1st of 1939 it happened. At 4:45am, 1 ½ million German troops amassed along the entire 1,750 mile Polish border. The German Luftwaffe bombed Polish airfields and the German navy attacked our naval forces in the Baltic Sea.

Hitler was worried about the Russians coming to the aid of the Poles if his forces attacked Poland, so he signed a non-aggression pact with the Soviet Union on August 23rd. As a precursor to the attack on the 1st, Hitler's S.S. troops wearing Polish uniforms staged a phony invasion of Germany the night before. They damaged several minor installations on the German side of the border. They also left behind a handful of dead concentration camp prisoners in Polish uniforms as evidence of the supposed Polish invasion.

The Polish army of one million men were mobilized but were outmatched by the superior German forces. By September 8th, the Germans reached the outskirts of Warsaw; they had advanced 140 miles in just one week! Brave Polish troops held out as long as they could, but when the Soviets invaded from the east on September 17th, all hope was lost, though Poland didn't officially capitulate until September 28th. For the fourth time in our history Poland was once again partitioned, now between Germany and the Russians.

Chapter II
My world changes

The invasion of tiny Gostynin was less forceful but every bit as dramatic as the conquests of larger cities. When the German army entered Gostynin in September there were immediate mass arrests of Jews and property was looted and destroyed. Our synagogue (which was rebuilt after a fire which occurred forty years earlier) was ordered to be dismantled. The wood was to be used for fuel for the German inhabitants of our town. There were many forms of repression.

On a personal level, I was nearly fifteen years old in 1939 and was working in a barbershop as an apprentice in Zychlin. I walked outside and was leaning on the wall of the shop when a good looking man in uniform said to me, "Bist du Jude?" (Are you a Jew?) I said, quite innocently, "Yes." The man hit me so hard that he split my lip. I went dizzy. He grabbed me by the collar and paraded me over to the nearby shoemaker and told me to take off his jackboots for him. I remember being humiliated and very angry. How could such a handsome man in uniform treat me this way? It just didn't make sense to me.

Then I saw the other Germans coming, heading for the barbershop. I also saw uniformed soldiers wearing black leather on motorcycles. One stopped and rubbed the bearded face of an old Jewish man in the dirt. It didn't take a genius to know that evil was on the march.

Everyone was afraid to talk about what was going on with the Germans. It was a taboo subject. No information was forthcoming from any quarter. We were all in the dark...and terrified.

Concentration and extermination camps
in occupied Poland

We had to leave the barbershop, Zychlin and move to the ghetto. People were confused and frightened beyond belief. The Germans were going house-to-house, rounding up people. Finally they came to my grandparents' house. My uncles, who were experienced in the ways of the military asked the Germans to leave me alone. They did, but they took my uncles, instead, to work in the slaughterhouse. We were all moved to the ghetto, and my uncles would come back there at night after their work in the slaughterhouse was done. There was also a big factory nearby, owned by Brown Bouveri, a Swiss company.

That fateful first day in September, German dive bombers made their runs. I will never forget the whine of the Stuka dive bomber engines as they dove closer and closer to earth. It was otherworldly. They hit the railroad station, knocking out any hope of escape by rail.

Exorbitant fines were levied against our Jewish community. They were ordered to pay two *contributions* (a nice word for a forced and totally unwarranted fine) in succession. When the president of the community was unable to collect the second sum in time, he sent a delegation to the Warsaw Jewish community and they gave him the required amount to hand over to the Nazis.

Jews were forced into smaller and smaller residences in one section of the village, but the property confiscation wasn't the worst of it. There were multiple killings and rapes. All Jews were commanded to wear yellow patches with the 'Jude' star on them. We were forbidden to walk on our own sidewalks, only allowed on the streets. Every time a Nazi in uniform would pass we had to remove our hats for him. It was an awful time for my friends and I. We truly felt like prisoners in our own community...and we were!

We lived in houses in the ghetto, not in our own home and had to wear the yellow triangle patch on our backs. They set up a 'Judenrat' (Jewish Council) which was our 'mouthpiece' to interact with the Germans. We knew it was just a formality and couldn't effect any real change. It was cold in our houses, and the 'Kachelofen' (a ceramic heater) was incapable of heating our space properly because wood was scarce and what there was of it was going to German families instead of us in the ghetto. We were given food rations, not nearly enough to sustain us.

The Germans needed able-bodied men, so the next item on the Nazis' agenda was forced labor. Many of us were chosen to clean the streets, to care for the Germans' horses, to cut wood, etc. When the work was too hard and we fell to our knees out of exhaustion or made mistakes, they beat us, not with an open hand but with anything they could find.

I left the ghetto in Zychlin in late summer of 1940. I escaped and just walked to my parents' home in Gostynin - a full 25 miles away. It took me a half day. I took the yellow triangle off that marked me as a Jew before I entered the town. It was noticeably locked down. I reached our house, and it was occupied by 12 people, people from other communities. My parents embraced me, joyously, and asked me all about Zychlin and the relatives and the ghetto.

Later, in 1941, my parents were moved to the ghetto in Gostynin which was packed to overflowing. People in uniforms were parading about and intimidating everyone. One night, a guard pushed my mother with the butt of his rifle. Instinctively, I jumped to my mother's defense. At that moment, he turned the rifle on me, putting it right up to my chest. He laughed throughout the ordeal and said to himself, "Killing a Jew? There's no penalty for that." He then left.

The ghetto in Gostynin in 1939

Remnants of the Gostynin ghetto today

Another time in the early fall of 1940, I saw the guards marching a long line of townspeople to the site of the synagogue, and then they just shot them, just like that. Then they burned the building to the ground. Such brutality. It was surreal. We were running around with buckets of water trying to put out the fire, but the fire had already taken its toll.

There was no such thing as 'normal' anymore. The Germans and the guards were always trying to keep us off balance and instill fear in us. They needn't have tried so hard; we were already petrified of what the next day might bring. I had a friend who was an agriculturist and he and I planted some flowers. They were arranged beautifully and were a reminder that there was still some beauty left in the world, that was until the guards stomped on them.

My friend and I saw them do this from the soccer field where we were playing, but to do anything to stop them would have been pointless. It would have only ended in the guards turning their anger towards us. We were also worried about our families. If a guard couldn't get to you, he would seek out your family and make them the target. The anger was reaching the boiling point among those of us in our excitable teenage years. We wanted to get weapons and kill them all. In our hearts we knew this would never happen, but that didn't stop us from wishing it would.

I remember several events in the winter of 1940. I was told to go to the graveyard to dismantle a gravestone of a very righteous Jewish person. This was very painful for me. I was very afraid, but I hit the stone as ordered and it fell backwards. On the way home, I felt like I was being followed. It was the 'Kreis Amtsleiter' (a local district official). I remember his name. It was Wagner.

He was on his way to a restaurant. He called out to me, "Junge" (boy) and told me to come over to him. "Didn't you see my uniform?" "Yes," I answered. "Then why didn't you remove your cap? Give me your name. I want to see you in my office tomorrow morning." When I got home, I told my father who then went to the Judenrat to intercede for me. The man from the Judenrat said, "Don't worry, Krajcer, I'll go with him. Nothing will happen. I will just bribe the Kreis Amtsleiter and that will be that."

When the Judenrat representative and I showed up at the Kreis Amtsleiter's office he said, "What are you doing here with this boy? I don't need you here!" He took me into another room, past a German woman who was writing something and he hit me in the head so hard that I lost my balance. He told me to get out, but I was so dizzy and disoriented that I couldn't find the door. Instead of pointing me in the right direction he hit me again. That man left an indelible mark on me, not physically, but mentally. I will never forget that sadistic Kreis Amtsleiter, Wagner.

During that same bitter cold winter I was walking with two friends. We had been shoveling snow all day, and to make the time pass on the way home we sang patriotic Polish songs. We also sang 'La Marseillaise,' the French national anthem, because the Nazis hated it. Upon hearing us singing, a Nazi officer took my name and said I had to come to his office the following day. I thought about what fate might befall me all that night, remembering my encounter with KA Wagner. I tossed and turned in bed thinking the worst.

When I woke up my sheets were wet with perspiration. I got up, still shaking with fear, dressed myself and walked to the building where the German officer worked. I entered, and as swiftly as can be, he hauled off and hit me on my head.

He said this was for disrespecting the Third Reich. This was not an isolated event. Many Jews, who were easily identified by the 'Jude' star, were routinely kicked, spat upon, beaten and belittled by the Germans. To the Nazis, it was sport or some kind of retribution for some imaginary ill they had suffered or perhaps it was out of allegiance to the Fuhrer's 'Aryan supremacy' ideology.

Another explanation could be that they needed an easily conquerable enemy, and we were readily available. I don't know. The evil actions of men are often hard to explain, but as I was beginning to see, they were real and viciously brutal and could flare up at any time.

In January, 1941, two things happened right after another: the Germans set up a ghetto in Gostynin. It occupied the area of Plocka, Buczka, Wojska Polskiego and Bagnista Streets and the next was the Germans were moving people to work camps. In the beginning, the ghetto was open, without any barbed wire, but that was soon to change. There was only one gate, and it was guarded by Jewish police and sometimes by German authorities.

It was filled to the brim with approximately 3,500 Jews. Many were employed in laundering and tailoring workshops. The ghetto, itself, was a small collection of buildings. Our family lived in an apartment with only two rooms and a kitchen, along with 14 other people. Sanitation wasn't fit for animals let alone humans. There was no running water. Despite that, we tried our best to keep it clean. Food was another big problem. There was very little of it and the situation worsened with each passing day. It was there that I learned what real hunger was like for the first time in my life. My uncle, Icze and I crept out at night to buy food from Polish friends.

The food was very expensive, and we carried it all back to the ghetto which was very dangerous, indeed. If caught, we would have been beaten...or worse. We did this a couple of times a week and sold the excess food to other people at a low price. We felt a moral obligation to help others stay alive.

In the spring of 1941, the Nazis decided to take young Jewish men from the ghetto to work camps outside the ghetto. Many of us suspected that this was a ruse to just remove us and kill us, away from the eyes of our families (word of mass executions in *Vernichtungslager* - death camps - had not reached us at this point). These selections were made during the daytime hours.

Fearing for their lives, many tried to escape, and some did, successfully, but not for long. The Gestapo caught them and returned them to the camp and hung them before everyone, leaving them dangle there as a grim reminder of our fate should we to try to escape. They made a grisly example of them. I remember the men's names: Berel Naiman, Mendel Mair and his brother Nachum. Berel was a cousin of Mendel Mair and Nachum. May they all rest in peace.

The Nazis were always improving and varying their methods. They started making their roundups in the night, taking the men away by force. Needless to say, those that were taken away never returned. In one of the roundups, they grabbed me, some of my friends and men we didn't know. They walked us outside the ghetto and put us in an L-shaped building. Nazi policemen were pacing around, watching for any sign of escape moves. Inside, a group of my friends and I were the last in line. Soldiers seated at tables were registering everyone's name. When they came to us, some of my friends began to cry. Others were scared out of their wits and nearly lost their senses. I was scared, too, but I was determined to escape.

SS executing Polish prisoners in Gostynin

One of the boys who was crying told me that he was staying because he knew his father would come and bribe the guards to set him free. When you're young and fearing for your life you don't necessarily think things through. All I knew was that if I stayed I'd be marked for death and that was not an option. I walked carefully and slowly to the window not to attract attention. I stopped, abruptly, as a policeman walked by. I waited for a minute and then quietly opened the window and escaped through it.

The *runner* in me took over and I must have broken the land speed record while I ran through the streets to a nearby building for temporary safety and then to an orchard. I didn't want to waste any energy or time so I rarely looked back. At a point, I did turn around, and seeing no one chasing me, I stopped, took off the yellow 'Jude star' that branded us as Jews and buried it under some soft dirt near a tree.

Not wanting to go back to the ghetto where a patrol or at least a guard would be looking for me, I decided to try my parents' old house, but when I arrived, our old landlord was there and he told me to go, to run, that it wasn't safe, so I decided to head for my grandparents' house in the Zychlin ghetto, 25 miles southeast of Gostynin. This was a very dangerous road for a Jewish boy to take. It was particularly dangerous for one that was being hunted without his yellow star. I felt that I had no choice.

To get there I had to walk through side roads in the direction of the ghetto. At one point, Polish boys ran after me screaming, "Jew, Jew" and threw stones at me. I threw the stones back at them and shifted into a higher gear and ran very fast away from them. Finally, I reached the Jewish cemetery. I walked and ran for what seemed like an eternity until I saw the Zychlin ghetto in the distance.

The gates were closed so I ran to the ditch that formed the outer boundary of the ghetto. I jumped it and boldly walked into the ghetto. Looking back, this was a very risky move as no Jewish person was allowed outside the ghetto and anyone trying to get IN would be grabbed and interrogated.

I managed to reach my relatives' small apartment and entered it. At once, my grandparents, uncles and aunts were all kissing and hugging me. "How can a child like you do this in such dangerous times?" they said. They gave me a little food, very little, since they didn't have much, themselves. They queried me about everybody and everything. I told them my story about the escape and they were very concerned. I said they shouldn't worry, that I would be very careful and everything would be all right (something I, myself, had trouble believing).

I kept myself concealed, and two days later, very early in the morning, after a dramatic goodbye, I left Zychlin. Though I didn't know for sure, I suspected that this was our final farewell. We would never see each other again. God rest their souls.

I trekked back to the ghetto in Gostynin and returned home, thinking that the guards had stopped looking for me. This was a happy day for the family, seeing me back and well. They thought that I was sent to the work camp and that they would never see me again.

My family had many Polish friends from whom they had bought provisions and livestock in the past. My father would go out twice a week from the ghetto and buy live chickens and other food to bring back to the ghetto for sale. We had a specialist in kosher slaughtering who would kill them and afterwards my brothers and I would dress them, plucking their feathers.

These evening excursions beyond the ghetto were very dangerous and I told my father that I should go because I was quicker (the 'runner', you know). After discussing my offer with my mother he agreed, so I took his place. I would go out three times a week; it was best when the moon was in its first phases. Less light, less chance of getting nabbed by the guards.

In the early spring evenings, young boys and girls came together in a dark corner of the ghetto. We had serious discussions about what might happen to us. Should we escape? To where? The odds were not in our favor. What to do? There seemed to be no good solution. We couldn't mount an attack against the German guards. We had no weapons and most of us didn't know how to use them, anyway. In the ghetto, people were getting sicker and sicker from hunger. There were fewer and fewer young people. It was a desperate situation.

Many significant events occurred in that summer of 1941. We lived close to the fence that surrounded the ghetto. The river was nearby. In the late summer and early fall, they took two transports of young women to the camps, and one day I saw two young men outside the ghetto standing around debating what they should do. I asked them if they were Jews. They said, "Yes," so I asked them to come in. When I think back, this was brave of them, not knowing what lay on the other side of the fence.

They related a story about Chelmno, how the Nazis were killing Jewish people and taking everything from them before they did. "They stripped them all of their clothes and put them in steel plate-covered trucks and they pumped in some lethal gas. They drove them to newly-dug graves and threw the dead bodies in.

"Everybody around the table felt that this was impossible. People could not do such a thing! The world would not permit this to happen. The two men told us that it was true. One of them said, "It will happen here, also.""

My family said, "Don't tell these stories. They are not true!" The young men said, "You will be charged for the transportation to your own death!" This shocked and worried everyone in the house, and when I went to bed that night I put my boots a few inches closer to me than usual, to be ready, just in case.

We were many in the same room and the nervousness was palpable. It was maybe 9:00 or 10:00 pm when one of my uncles opened the door and was screaming, "They're coming. they're grabbing people." I took what clothes I could find, pulled on my boots and ran out of the house. The Germans chased me past many buildings, so I jumped up on a roof. I ran from roof to roof until I found a place where three roofs converged and jumped down to the second roof making myself as inconspicuous and small as possible. I was well hidden, and from my vantage point could see that the soldiers were beating the people below me. After a few tortuous minutes, and when I saw that the coast was clear, I jumped down and ran back to my house.

The Germans found us and nabbed my father, his brother Icze, myself and some other Jewish people. They put us in a building with steel bars on the windows and no apparent way of escaping. My father and uncle Icze talked among themselves about what they should do, and then a truck arrived and the guards started moving people out to the truck. In the beginning, the Germans were not well organized. My uncle saw an opening and he escaped in the confusion. I was the last one in line.

A Nazi was sitting on the truck behind a machine gun. I then did something I will never regret. I begged the Nazis to let my father go. I told them that I would go in his place. Having never having heard this kind of impertinence from a Jew before he asked, "What?" I repeated what I said. He took out a whip and started to beat me with it.

It didn't matter to me that he was armed, was bigger and more powerful. This was my father's life we were fighting over, and I adamantly refused to go on the truck! He was getting angrier by the second.

That's when he threw me to the ground. He kicked me and beat me, but this little Jewish boy still refused. I was so stubborn that I told him to go ahead and kill me. I was not going on that truck unless he let my father go home. All this time my father was very scared. He begged me to get on the truck and said that we would go together. I said, "No" in the loudest way possible. Finally, the soldier told my father to go home, and I went to the truck and sat at the end in the corner.

The soldier ordered everybody to sit still with their heads bowed to their knees. He said that if anyone lifts his head he will blow it off. This was an open truck, the height of the sides were approximately two to three feet high. The truck started moving along the road near the ghetto fence. All of a sudden I saw my mother running with two bundles for us. At that very moment something happened to me...I knew I had to escape. Instinct took over; there was no time for a plan. When the truck crossed a little bridge at the next curve I jumped off. The moment my feet touched the ground the runner in me appeared. Throwing caution to the wind and with the wind at my back I ran very fast to a house which was situated on an open space along the river.

To my surprise, nobody was chasing me! Fear and a sense of uncertainty gripped me. I was afraid to go home, so I decided to wait out the adrenaline that was pumping through my system. Twenty minutes later, I walked carefully back to the ghetto. I crawled under the barbed wire fence into the ghetto and then on to my parents' apartment.

It is impossible to describe the feeling in that tiny house when my father and mother saw me. They were crying, uncontrollably, from happiness. They were kissing and hugging me as were my two younger brothers, uncles and aunts and grandfather. They treated me like a hero, like General Pilsudski himself! To think, a boy was ready to sacrifice his life, unbelievable! After the sounds of happiness in our house died down, we all heard moaning and crying coming from a neighbor's house. The Germans had taken away the woman's husband and her son. In other houses there were similar cries of pain. The night wouldn't be silent.

We were living on borrowed time, all of us. From day to day things got progressively worse. The war news was very depressing. The Nazis had conquered Europe from Spain to the Volga River. There was no hope for us.

Then they came for my father and his brother-in-law. My brothers hid in the basements. The women of the family and my uncle came together and made a decision to flee to the ghetto in Warsaw. They immediately started sewing gold and other valuables into their clothing. We found a man that would take us over the border as we were certain that the end was coming for the Jews of Gostynin. We were to meet the man in a field. He would have horses for us. I took the hand of a young delicate girl who was with us and guided her to the field in the darkening skies of the early evening.

When we got to the agreed-upon spot we were met by three fairly well-to-do women from our village. They started to scream that we should escape, that the Germans were there. They took our money and we ran. There were no Germans. It was all just a trick to steal our money.

My uncle led us back to Gostynin through the dark forest road. All of a sudden a Polish person with a whistle said, "Halt! I must call the German guards!" While this was happening the women were all crying. My uncle turned to me and said, "It's his life or ours Yitzak."

Fortunately for the man, he thought better of blowing his whistle and let us go. It was clear to my uncle that such a large group as ours would be at risk. We needed to split up. At that point, we came upon a Polish boy on his bicycle who recognized me and said that we should go in a different direction, that the German police were behind him. I immediately jumped into the thicket but the women were too slow and they were captured and taken to the police station, stripped of their valuables and returned to the ghetto.

We followed, but at a distance. The ghetto remained our home for a few more months. Then, we were told that we would all soon be leaving for the work camps. In the beginning of the winter of 1941/42, grandfather died. We buried him in the Jewish cemetery. I remember that people were saying how lucky he was to have died in his own bed. We sat Shiva in the ghetto for him. I was not allowed to go to the funeral for fear they would take me to the work camp. The apartment was freezing cold and there was little hope and even less food. At the beginning of 1942, the Nazis told the Jewish representative that all men able to work must register to work. This was the only way to survive. All the men went. From our family, my brother, uncles and cousins were chosen.

Again, I managed to escape with uncle Icze. We found a Polish friend of his that took us in for awhile. The next day, Jewish people from all over the country were taken to the railroad station. They came from Gostynin, Gombin and Saniki. I think almost 900 people left.

It was then that a most amazing thing happened in Konin. There were about 50 persons left, awaiting their turn, but instead of passively waiting, they decided to form an uprising. It failed. The Nazis took some 40 of them to work camps. The ten left behind were told to spread petrol all over the camp and burn it down. They did as they were told, but instead of giving the Nazis the satisfaction of killing them, they hung themselves.

We heard from neighboring ghettos that they took most everybody to Chelmno, west of Warsaw. We knew we were next. Mother told me that I had a duty to escape with uncle Icze. My mother, along with my youngest brother and my aunts would stay together. "There was no other choice, " she said. "Escape while you can." Separation was painful and dramatic. Mother kissed and hugged me and we were all crying. She literally pushed me out the door and told me to run and Godspeed. That was the last time I saw my mother and little brother. On April 12, 1942 they were taken to Chelmno.

Nobody from my family, not my father nor my mother or my brothers, survived. I am the only one left, and I said to myself, "If I am to survive, I must learn to live in the shadows of the worst tyranny man has ever known." All of my dear family are in my daily thoughts. I miss them as much today as I did when we parted. That sort of pain never goes away.

The ghetto of Zychlin was liquidated at the end of 1941. Gostynin was liquidated in April of 1942.

37

Most of the remaining 2,000 inhabitants were deported to the Chelmno extermination center near the village of Chelmno-nad-Ner (west of Warsaw and north of Lodz). The rest were taken to the Lodz Ghetto and the Konin Concentration Camp)

According to Shmuel Ben Eliezer of the Jewish Press, "There are no Jewish residents in Gostynin today. There are a number of memorials, however, to the former Jewish community of Gostynin. One large marble plaque is in the Chamber of the Holocaust Memorial Museum on Mount Zion in Jerusalem. Gostynin is included in the "Valley of Communities" memorial at Yad Vashem, also in Jerusalem. A *Yizkor* book for Gostynin, <u>*Pinkas Gostynin,*</u> was published in 1961 as a joint publication of the New York and Israel Gostynin *landsmann* groups. Only the Israeli Gostynin *landsmann* group exists today."

Like many Jewish cemeteries, the cemetery in Gostynin was desecrated and destroyed. The tombstones were hauled away and presumably broken up by the Nazis. The tomb (ohel) of the local zaddik (a zaddik is a title given to a Jewish man who is especially righteous and pious) was destroyed. The few Jews from Gostynin who survived the Holocaust subsequently emigrated. I am one of them.

Chapter III
The shadows fall

After a dangerous journey, uncle Izce and I came to the ghetto, Strzegowo, which is about 25 kilometers west of Warsaw and close to the Prussian border. It was a small ghetto run by a decent Jewish person. When we arrived, there was no place for us to sleep, but we managed. My uncle did find us a bed that would fit us both. One day, the Germans came for me and put me in a wagon and drove me to a large sugar factory where farmers brought their sugar beets for processing. I was set to the task of digging peat. I went from farm to farm for months, digging. The farmers were very kind to all of us and they taught me about plowing. In the spring/summer of 1942, the Germans told us that we would now be digging sugar beets.

They took us back to the ghetto, but we knew they had something else in mind for our future. They were rushing to get rid of us and using any excuse to kill Jews. I remember a well-dressed woman from Gostynin say to me, "You go to the back of the line and I will stay in the front." Everybody was telling me in their own way to go, to escape. If I heard, "You will survive" once, I heard it a dozen times over.

The last night in the ghetto was enormously tension-filled. Everybody knew that this was their last night, the last hours of their lives. In our room lived my uncle, four couples (two of them had small girls) and a teenage girl. It was a cold, windy and dark night and the ghetto was surrounded by Nazi guards with weapons. The ghetto was sealed off, completely, no one could get in or out. The couples with children were holding hands, hugging and crying while their children slept. The other two couples and the teenage girl were also crying.

Watching this made me terribly upset and I had to leave the room. It was simply too much to bear. By chance, I walked into another house where people were praying. I was stunned at the intensity of their prayer as they chanted and cried, begging to God for their lives. One of the boys said that there was some money hidden in a wall. "Come," he said. "We can take it and strike out on our own." I told him that I was going with my uncle.

Overwhelmed, I had to leave the building. I went back to the room in my house and saw that nothing had changed, except for the sobbing which got louder. There was intermittent discussion between sobs and the subject of escape came up. My uncle realized that the families would not separate from one another and that would make their escape, impossible.

We told them of our decision to escape and they wished us good luck and gave us some money, gold chains and other valuables to helps us. They begged us not to forget them. One of the women, a Mrs. Izbicka, put her hand on my face and assured me, "You will survive. Don't forget us, ever, and don't forget to tell what happened to us." It was an emotional separation for both of us. Soon it would be light and we needed to leave. We saw wagons coming to take people to the camps. Quietly, we walked to the last house in the ghetto and then crawled to avoid being seen by the guards.

My uncle managed to get us out, past the hanging field where the Germans executed people, but that was just the first step. I know it sounds crazy, but we decided to head back to Gostynin, along a very dangerous road. My uncle had the name of a farmer at whose house we could stay along the way. It was now 3:00 am.

We eventually got to the farmer's house and asked him if we could stay overnight. We said we would pay. Fortunately for us he agreed. His wife made us some food, and afterwards we slept in the barn. During these times, everyone slept with one eye open and not for very long, either. After a few hours of sleep, uncle Icze and I left. I remember that it was a cold dark night.

We came to a farming village, not far from the town of Raciaz and knocked on the door of a farmer's house. This house was isolated, quite a distance from the other houses, so we felt reasonably safe. The farmer and his wife were friendly people. They told us we could stay and rest for a few days. We slept in their barn and ate in the house. We paid them for their hospitality. One day, a Nazi soldier came to take inventory of the farm. This caught all of us unawares. We literally had no time to escape so we were told to hide between the closet and a wall! The farmer's wife was very clever...and calm.

She asked the soldier to sit down at a table some twenty feet away from us. He stayed a few minutes, writing down things in his notebook, and then she invited him outside, to take a look around the farm. He later drove away. This was a dangerous moment for us, the farmer and his wife, and we all felt as if someone had ripped open our stomachs and emptied the contents on the table.

In the evening, the farmer had a proposition. He said, that for 1,000 Reich Marks, he would arrange to send me to work in Germany as a substitute for a Polish boy. My uncle would have to leave, though. We talked over the situation, the separation. Again, we felt that we had no choice and agreed. Uncle gave him the money (a thousand Marks was quite a large sum in those days).

We had a feeling that this would be the last time we would see each other for a long time. I gave my uncle the rest of our money and other things. The goodbye was a dramatic one, hugging, crying, wishing good luck to each other. *His luck didn't last long. Uncle Icze was killed by the Nazis in Gostynin in 1943. A Polish farmer informed on him.*

The very next day, the farmer took me to a family whose son got a call to go to Germany. This was common, as the Nazis conscripted Poles to work for them. It was planned that I would substitute for him, as we were both the same age. I had an official paper as a travel document. The farmer went back to his home. In the evening, the new family changed their minds. They didn't want to take the risk with their son.

In the event that the Germans found out, they would come to their house and kill them all, so they told me to leave their home. I went back to the first farmer's house.

The following day, he hitched up the horse and wagon and took me to yet another family. Their son was also supposed to go to Germany. Again, he made the same arrangement as before. This family was glad that they could send a substitute for their son. I was happy, too. The farmer was relieved, I think, and he went home. My new 'adopted' family gave me the call-up document and I had to remember all the information on it such as place of birth, etc.

They gave me a package of food and clothing to take with me. I remember being both happy and afraid. That night, I slept in a room in a real bed. In the early hours of the morning, they were shaking me and screaming. They told me to get out of the house immediately because "You are a Jew! you are a Jew!"

They threatened to call the Germans. Scared, I fled their house and ran out into the black night, through fields and forest. I headed in the direction of the first farmer's house. It was quite a distance away, and I remember stumbling around in the darkness. I arrived there, not to be greeted with open arms, but to frustration and anger. He was not happy to see me. He drove me away to a forest.

At this point, I didn't know if he had decided to do me in, but luckily, he took me to an old house deep in the forest. Inside was a man with the long red beard. He sat beside a big porcelain Kachelofen (heater) with a fire. He took the man aside and they spoke in whispers. Afterwards, he told me that this was the best place for me to survive. I was worried that they were plotting to get rid of me. I pleaded with the farmer to please, please take me back with him. Reluctantly, he did, but when we arrived back at his farm he told me once again that I would have to leave his house. This was maddening! I kept going over the events in my mind.

"How did they know that I was Jewish?" I thought the only way was that they had peeked under my bedcovers and saw that I was circumcised (all Jewish men are circumcised).

Our tradition of circumcision was a telltale sign of our religion and a sure passport to death. When I left the farm, he gave me some advice, some food but not a penny for my journey. Totally on my own, now, I don't mind admitting that I was plenty scared. No one had to tell me that my life was in big danger. Danger was everywhere, and I was sure that my chances of survival were slim, at best.

Wandering from place to place was not an option. Sooner or later someone would notice me or figure out that I was a Jew, and I could no longer avoid capture. I could not survive long. I don't know when it hit me, but I had the strangest feeling, comforting in a way. I decided that what happens to all Jewish people would happen to me though I didn't want to be killed like an animal.

I would test my fate and travel to the Warsaw ghetto. This journey, too, was fraught with peril, along even more dangerous roads. I was on the side of Poland that was in the Third Reich. Warsaw was a protectorate. There was a border to cross, the Narew River, and I was determined to get there. Some farmers, not knowing that I was Jewish, gave me advice and some food. I was walking through fields, forests and side roads, zigzagging my way.

Finally, I got to within a few kilometers from the village of Glinojeck which was 100 kilometers northwest of Warsaw. There was a big sugar factory there and many Nazis lived around the village. This was a very dangerous place for a Jewish person to be so I changed direction and headed towards another, safer village and other farms. I found a friendly farmer who offered to feed me and give me some assistance, but as soon as he opened his door, his wife was crying and told me to have mercy on them and leave, immediately.

"There are many Germans around the village," she kept repeating. She feared for her own children. I understood and left the farm. Another farmer saw me walking and called me to his house. He gave me bread and coffee and advised me which roads to take. I thanked him. I was back on the road to nowhere.

In the evening, it was getting darker and colder. I knew I had to find a place - any place - to sleep. In the next village was a much larger farm than the others. A Polish person managed it for the Germans. I managed to persuade the man that I was a hard worker and wouldn't be any trouble for him if only he would take me on as a laborer.

To my delight, he did. I did all manner of manual labor and got to be very friendly with the manager and other workers there. Before the war, I was learning the barbering trade and I still had some barber tools with me.

After work in the evenings, the manager and some people asked me to cut their hair and shave them. I was always given food for my services and I made some friends. The food I shared with three girls and four boys. (None of them survived.) I went to the home of the manager, thinking maybe I could stay overnight with them. When I walked in, the wife was alone in the kitchen. She was a very pleasant person, very friendly. In the next room were two grown daughters and a boyfriend of one of them. The woman started to prepare food for me. I asked where the husband was.

He was sick and in another room, she told me. She thought he would be glad to see me. When he saw me, he started to scream that I should leave the main house because I was endangering their lives! He told me to leave, immediately. The wife took me back to the kitchen and gave me something to eat and drink. The boyfriend came in and stared at me. "You Jew, go away from here. I will call the Germans," he said. "They will take you away," he continued. The woman told him to leave me alone. "Not in my house and not in my lifetime," she said. She told me not to worry, that nothing would happen to me there.

She took down a kerosene lantern from a shelf and walked with me to a very big barn with many cows. She told me to climb up to the loft, cover myself completely with hay, and to try to be calm. She would come for me early the next morning and wake me up. It was wet and cold so I kept my boots on. I slept, fitfully, the day's events swirling around in my mind like some kind of awful carousel.

It was still dark when she woke me up. She gave me food and wished me the best, blessed me, said to go save myself and good luck. Things like this you don't forget. You remember kindnesses like this all your life.

I walked and walked in the direction of Warsaw, but I got lost. Suddenly, I smelled fresh bread. I followed the smell to a house and was invited in by a farmer. He said that I could have some bread and that his son would be leaving the farm the next morning and I could go with him in the direction of Warsaw. The next morning was a Sunday and I awoke early, had some coffee and bread and set out with the farmer's son. After a kilometer or two we stopped by a ditch. The boy said, "You are a Jew. Give me everything you have."

At that, we started fighting and two German hunters with shotguns appeared. When the boy saw them he got really scared as he couldn't understand German, but I did. They said, "You stupid boys, these are hunting grounds. You could get killed. Leave this place!" Fortunately, this stopped our fight and I told the boy I was not a Jew so we continued to walk until we came to a forest. We had reached the house of the boy's aunt. Before he entered he gave me directions to the river. I walked for some time until I reached it. I saw some people hiding in the bushes near the river.

Tired, I sat down and a boy came up to me and said, "You're a Jew." I said, "I'm a Jew like you're a Jew," and he ambled off, muttering to himself.

I decided that if worse came to worse I would swim to the other side of the river if only to escape more accusations of being a Jew! It was only a few minutes later when the same boy came by; he was relaxed and probably convinced that I wasn't a Jew after all. I was now sitting with some other people, so I didn't expect a scene from him. Pretty soon an older man came by, wheezing terribly. Another man also came by and the boy told him (pointing to me) "Here's somebody that could carry the old man's load."

We started a conversation. He explained that in the night, fishermen in small boats would take people across, but they didn't do it for free. You had to pay them. This was not the information I was hoping for considering I had no money. He said that some people also cross with food they will sell in Warsaw on the black market. My mind went back to my father and all the times he had sold provisions in Warsaw. I felt a tinge of sadness. I still missed him, greatly.

Later, the wheezing man said he could no longer carry the bundle and I was elected to take his place after I convinced the leader of the group that I could manage carrying a heavy bundle of meat. The little boat arrived and we all ran down to the river. We jumped into the boat with bundles. We were the first ones on board. A few more people came and the fishermen took us across the river.

We grabbed up the bundles and jumped out of the boat into the water and started to run, fast. Suddenly the crack of rifle fire split the night. We heard shots and screams from the other side.

We ran a long way and then, momentarily out of breath, we stopped to rest on the moist ground. A few minutes of catching our breath and I closed my eyes. The others thought that I was asleep and they started to talk about me. "That such a young boy was doing such a good job." They felt sorry for me.

Our group headed for the forester's house with our bundles. There we were ushered into a large cozy room. I remember how nice and warm it was. We were served food and drink and downed it all with great relish. A man came over to me and asked if I wanted to continue on to Warsaw. I said, "Yes," and the next morning we headed off to the train station in Legionowo, north of Warsaw.

We boarded the train and I heard young Polish people singing a familiar song but with different words: "In Saski Park near the fountain, you don't see more Jewish girls. The Sallys and Esthers don't live anymore among us. They're wandering in another sphere." It was painful to hear. Soon, we were in Warsaw at the Gdansk Station and me without papers of any kind! My stomach clenched up into a ball. I had a terrible feeling. I couldn't get the 'Saski Park' song out of my mind.

In such horrible times, these people were singing, laughing and joking about the fate of Jewish people. The Polish police separated the people with bundles from the rest of the group. The lead man with the bundle bearers went up to the police and told me to come with him. I'm pretty sure he bribed them. I heard him say, "Come on. Come on. This way." We boarded a tram and he took me to his home in Warsaw. It is now late in 1942, a full three years after the German occupation of Poland. This man was very nice to me and I think a little proud of me. He told his wife how I helped him cross the border with his merchandise.

He told me not to worry, to take a shower and get some sleep. I don't know how long I slept, but it must have been many hours. He woke me up and said, "Boy can you sleep!" We ate a full hot breakfast and he paid me for my service as a bundle-bearer. He also asked me what my plans were now that I was in Warsaw.

I said that I needed to make a living and find a place to live. I didn't know where the ghetto was, but that I could probably smuggle food there for some money. The man cautioned against it, that it was too dangerous. I thanked him for his kindness and took the tram he suggested, and he made me promise that I would take the route he outlined so as to avoid contact with the Germans.

His house was just outside of Warsaw and after the tram ride and a few hours on foot, I found the Warsaw ghetto and walked on the sidewalk across the street from it. The ghetto was surrounded by a big brick wall. There were Polish police and German police at strategic points along the wall. The road was opened to traffic, but it wasn't all civilian traffic. There were German patrols all over the city. It was a very dangerous place for a Jewish boy to be.

I had to decide what to do. I thought if I tried to get inside they would certainly kill me. If I do get in, I will probably starve to death. Something inside me nagged at me to go back to Gostynin. Why? I don't know for the life of me. Maybe some Polish friends could help me find some lodging in a safe place. I went to the central railroad station and bought a ticket to Lowicz, some 70 kilometers from Gostynin. I had no idea of the danger I was in.

During this time, the Nazis were looking for Jewish people all over, especially in Warsaw in the autumn of 1942. Polish and German police, the Gestapo and even some ordinary Polish citizens were hunting for Jews, demanding money from the Jews if they found them. If no blood money was possible, then they would turn you into the Gestapo for a reward.

The ghetto in Warsaw

To be treated like a criminal without committing a crime made me more and more angry. At the railroad station, the Germans were checking identification papers.

It was lucky for me that I arrived in Lowicz late in the afternoon. It was getting dark and the document check would end soon. It was also windy and cold and I was worried where I would spend the night. Walking out from the station, I saw a group of Polish boys.

I approached them and told them I escaped from the camp and that I needed help. The boys didn't know that I was Jewish otherwise they probably would have turned me away. One of them told me that certain people were looking for substitutes to go to Germany to work. He told me to head for the street (the name has long since escaped me) where the office was located and I would find those people looking for substitutes.

Again, my inner runner took over. I ran without stopping to this place. It was already dark and not many people were around. I asked two drunks leaning up against the building if they know someone looking for a replacement to go to work in Germany. They pointed to a man across the street and said, "Try him. Maybe he's looking for somebody."

I approached the man, carefully, because he could have been the SS or someone baiting a trap for unsuspecting people like me. I asked him if he was looking for a replacement for his son to go to Germany. He startled me when he grabbed my hand and said, "God sent you to me! I'll give you what you want." I was careful to stay calm and asked for clothing and shoes and told him I was hungry. We went to a restaurant and ate. He told me, that when we were in the office, I had to call him 'tata' or 'ojciec' (dad) and he would call me 'syn' (son).

He told me his son's birth date and place of birth. This I must commit to memory and not blurt out my own, instead. He promised to bring me everything I needed the next day. We went to the office where such boys were supposed to register. I was scared stiff, but everything went according to plan. We parted company. The German official took the call-up paper and gave me new papers with my new name which was Stanislaw Guragczik.

From this moment on I ceased to be Isaac Krajcer, Jewish boy from Gostynin. I was now a Polish gentile boy named Stanislaw. They sent me to a transit camp in Warsaw along with thousands of other boys and men where I encountered some problems with the Polish police being registered. Two of the officials took me to their office and asked if I was a replacement for someone and what my real name was?

I told them, "This is me, what do you want from me?" An officer came in and asked me the same thing and I gave him the same answer. They put me in the camp and gave me a place to lie down. After putting my things away, I put my feet up on the bunk and turned on my side. To my surprise, I saw a man from my hometown in Gostynin!

I was petrified that he might recognize me and give me away. He was an older person and didn't know me and just nodded when our eyes met. Very early in the morning they called my name and the names of many others. We were surrounded by police, and they took us to the train in Warsaw. Our destination was a big transit camp, Skaryszewska.

In barrack after barrack, the camp was full of thousands of mostly younger men. I was soon to experience my first serious problem. We all were told to strip naked so that our clothing could be disinfected.

I knew that that could be my unmasking as someone was bound to look at my genitals and see that I was circumcised.

We all lined up waiting for a medical examination. I was so scared. I felt my heart pounding out of my chest. I had to calm down and speak like nothing was wrong. I remember talking to myself. "This is the way to survive; don't give up." I closed ranks with the young man in front of me to obscure anyone's view of the front of my body.

I walked into a big hall with German military doctors. They checked me from head to toe and when the doctor checked my sex organ I felt like I would faint. It's not possible to express how I felt at this moment but I steeled myself. He didn't realize I was circumcised! After a while I tried to relax and move around in the shadows so no one would notice my 'condition.' I got my clothing back and dressed myself and tried to regain my composure.

I introduced myself to some other boys and started to make friends with them. I still had my shaving and barbering tools with me so I was busy giving shaves and making friends. After two days in this place, they took us to the railroad station. There were many guards watching for any attempts at escaping. We boarded a passenger train bound for Germany and traveled all night while many guards watched us until we arrived at the station in Zagan (or Sagan), Germany. The city is about 100 kilometers north of the border of the former Czechoslovakia.

Shortly after the invasion in 1939, the Germans established POW camps there. At one time over 300,000 prisoners from 30 different countries were incarcerated at that site. It is estimated that over 120,000 of them died of starvation, disease and maltreatment.

In March of 1942, the town became the site of 'Stalag Luft III' camp for captured airmen. I understand a film was made about this camp. It is called, 'The Great Escape.'

There were no more guards when we disembarked the train, and we were allowed to go out onto the ramp where they gave us coffee and bread. Then a strange thing happened. While walking on the ramp, I saw people with yellow patches on their backs working on the rails. I was drawn to them like a magnet and started to walk to the end of the ramp. Then I hesitated. I couldn't walk any closer. This was too dangerous for me. Contact with fellow Jews would draw attention to myself. Walking back to the train, my eyes were filled with tears.

Back on board we traveled through the night until we arrived in the city of Soest in the North Rhine-Westphalia district of Germany. This was an even bigger transit camp than the one we left behind. Again, same procedure. Off with our clothes for disinfection. I fooled them once. Could I fool them again? Being naked was dangerous for me.

Ukrainian Nazi collaborators put us in rows and started to spray us with disinfectant, all the time looking at us. I turned from side to side to avoid them. My friends and I hurried outside, running around playing games close to the gate. I saw a man near the gate with papers in a leather pouch. He called to me and asked me if I spoke German and did I want to work on the railroad. I said, "Yes." "You have friends?" "Yes." "Well, then, bring them here." I brought ten boys back and he took us out to the train. He said, "Take your things and come with me." All this time my *Jewishness* was hidden. We walked to the train station and boarded the train for Porta (it is now called, Porta Westfalica) in the district of Minden-Lübbecke.

It's on the Weser River, quite a beautiful place, actually. I wish I could say the same for the rail yards. The train stopped and we were handed off to an older man with a snowy white mustache and a loden green coat. He was friendly and spoke quietly to us. He said he would take us to the place where we would live. My first question to him was, "Is there a fence there?" He told me there was a fence and it was beautiful. We soon arrived at what was a large villa, three stories high. The house was just for railroad boys and the 'Hausmeister' (head of the property) was a railroad man, himself.

We were a mix of boys from several nationalities. There were Poles, Czechs, French, Dutch and Serbs. Hearing that I was Polish, the Poles asked, "What goes on in Poland? From what city do you come?" They peppered me with other questions too, but I had to be careful with my answers for fear that any one of them could have been a 'plant' sent by the Germans. They told me not to worry that this is a good place to be.

I was bunked up in a small room with another boy from Warsaw. They gave us blankets, linens and food for the rest of the week. Dinners we got from the kitchen. The next day we were driven to the police station to receive our identification papers. The policeman asked questions, but nobody understood German. He got aggravated so I told him that I spoke a little German. He said, "Ausgezeichnet (excellent). You are the interpreter." They took pictures of us with signs with numbers in front of us, and shortly thereafter we got our identification papers.

The very next day we started to work on the rail lines with other Polish men. I was checking on the ties. It was harder work than I was accustomed to. The other, older workers looked out for me. Some of them told the rail boss that this work was too hard for a young boy.

I remember one night they sent me on 'snow watch.' I was to keep an eye on the weather in case it snowed. Things needed to be kept free of ice, like the switches.

It was confusing to me at first - the new German words and the train terminology, but I learned, quickly. A short time later, they sent all of us newcomers to another station to work, except for my roommate and I. The months went by without incident. We settled into routines. Work. Eat. Sleep. Work. Eat. Sleep. Meals were plentiful and tasty. I remember looking forward to our supper. Christmas of 1942 came and we celebrated, all nationalities together. Later, I got a new job in a railroad dump yard where I worked with an old German man. Pretty soon my German improved because of our conversations together.

Some of us were there because our lands were occupied by the Germans; others were not. We Poles were supposed to wear a yellow, 'P' patch. The Russians had to wear 'Ost' (East) patches with white on blue. Though our movements were restricted, we were allowed to go outside.

I was the youngest boy in the house. One day, my roommate showed me a letter he got from his parents in Warsaw. The Jews were fighting the Germans, they said. The Germans were going from house to house, burning the buildings of the ghetto to the ground. The Jews jumped through windows. "They burned like bedbugs," was the expression the Germans used. To think that other human beings could be so callous about their fellow man. Of course, I had to remind myself that the Germans didn't consider us human. To them, we were nothing more than irritating insects that needed to be squashed under their boots. My roommate's parents had arranged for him to go back home, so I was moved to another room with other Polish men, some of them Jew-haters.

56

They told stories of kicking, beating and throwing rocks at 'the filthy vermin.' Warsaw was coming apart for the Jews while I was still hiding in plain sight. I was angry...and devastated...and filled with sadness, but had to keep it all inside. There were times when I simply had to leave the room and go stand outside to cool off.

Jews, and the trouble they were causing, was a common topic among those in the 'railroad house,' but I can remember one time when I heard the Landrat (a council member, named Malek) talk down the Jews only to be told to shut up - that "Now is not the time for that." Those rebukes were far from routine. Once I found a surprise in my closet. Someone had slipped me some sausage and other items. Later, I found out that the man who did it took pity on me for having so little in the way of possessions. His name was Leon, and he was what we call a 'mensch' (a true man).

Our work was often dangerous, too. We unloaded cars with building materials and had to clean the water tanks and take out the sludge. It was heavy work. Every time I felt exhausted I thought about all my Jewish friends who were in hiding or in work camps or worse. My discomfort was nothing compared to theirs. I had shelter, food and a job. I had no right to complain.

One day a friend told me we were to gather in a big room. The police were on their way to check if there were any Jews among us. "Oh, no. Not again!" I had to decide what to do. I had to show up or be conspicuous by my absence. We went to the room, and shortly the police arrived. I was scared and kept to myself. The police gave a speech, telling us to behave and work hard and to be sure to wear the Polish 'P' sign. Saved again. I didn't know how much more of this I could take, but over time I made my peace with it.

Life returned to normal or what passed for it. I formed friendships with many of the workers that were split up into two groups.

One group asked me to take a walk with them on Sundays. We talked about work, the war, the past, home. I was always careful what I said. I didn't push my luck. They didn't know I was Jewish and I wanted to keep it that way. I also managed to save up some money over time. I bought a jacket, pants, shoes, shirts and other things I needed. One day, a man came to my workplace. He was dressed in a railroad uniform and was a yardmaster. He was gruff and spoke in a clipped, sharp fashion.

A friend I was working with started up a conversation with him. The man approached me and said, "Boy this work is not for you. I'll arrange for you to come work with me in Minden, Westphalia at the railroad station there. I'll make you into a real railroad man."

You could have knocked me over with a feather. I was elated. Two other boys and myself were soon transferred to the railroad station in Minden, Westphalia to work. They called us to the office to explain what kind of work we would be doing and briefed us on the dangers. They said that we must be extra careful when crossing the tracks on the way home. We were to work on the yard, arranging freight cars, which was dangerous. We were to become shunters (locomotive car-switchers). They gave us railroad hats, working clothes and other things for work in day or night situations. My trainer was a partial invalid whose brother-in-law was an important man in the 'front office.' I was taught how to safely couple and decouple cars. I was a quick study. We worked in shifts, three Germans and one foreigner to each shift.

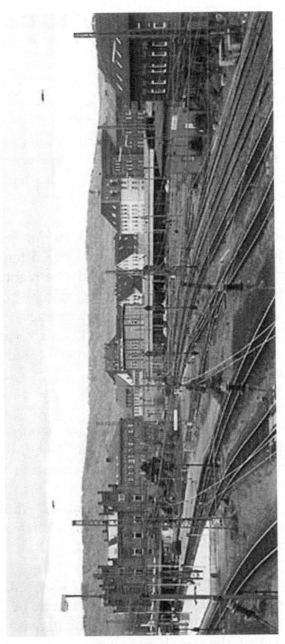

The train station in Minden

We lived with other Polish men and other nationalities. I started to make friends, also among the German-speaking members of the group.

I was more like a younger brother or nephew to some of them, I think. They called me, "Die Junge." (the young one) The trains were going everywhere: west to Cologne (some up to fifty cars long) and big trains full of commercial wares going east to Hanover. Every single car had to have documentation.

I had a good work ethic and a good reputation. The Germans liked the fact that I was always on time, and often early. We worked into the afternoon and through the night. I got my 'Dienst' (service) card with no nationality stamped on it, while the other Poles got 'Polnisch' stamped on theirs. Why mine was 'clean,' I don't know. I stuck the 'P' patch in my pocket and didn't wear it. I became more confident and felt more secure. That was a mistake.

We also unloaded cars, and there was a huge glass factory near the yard, and I remember loading an ungodly number of glass containers into the area that was called, the 'Hafen' (harbor) not because there was water there but because it was a central loading/off-loading area like a port. There were cars that came in with massive amounts of clothing from Russia, loaded with boots and underwear, taken from Russian POWs or from the 'camps.'

We had a rule; railroad car doors must be closed. I worked with a man named Karl Werner. Karl and I stood by the doors. Once the train lurched and I had my hand between the door and the wall of the car. It was wedged firmly and blood started to run from my hand. Karl took my hand and felt around the bones.

"Nothing broken," he assured me. "Just a flesh wound. Move your fingers," he said. It hurt like Hell when I did, but after wrapping it in a fresh handkerchief he told me to head for the hospital and have it checked out. A kindly nurse examined it, bandaged it properly and gave me a pass to stay off work for a few days.

I worked most of my time on the Deutsche Reichsbahn in Minden. Once, the railroad sent me to a 'Vertrauensarzt' (a doctor who examines patients who've been on sick leave for awhile). He checked my overall health and then dropped his attention to my genitals whereupon he said, "Gott in Himmel Herr Guragczik, Du bist Jude!" The doctor said I was Jewish because I was circumcised. That same moment something clicked in my head. If I don't object, he will know that I am. If I do object I have a chance, so I said, "Was sagen Sie? Ich bin kein Jude." (What are you saying? I'm no Jew.).

I could see that he was a cultured man so I spoke in measured tones, but firmly. I was insistent. I told him that I am Polish, that my parents were Polish and that I'm not a Jew. Then he said, "But why...?"

I told him that I couldn't answer that question so he said that he was going to send me to the 'Gesundheitsamt' (the Public Health Department). I left in a daze. Not again! Another opportunity to be found out. I was going crazy. There was no escape from his referral. When I got to the Gesundheitsamt, the place was full of propaganda pictures on the wall: Stalin, Roosevelt, Churchill with the text of 'warmonger' underneath each one. I had entered Hell's front door.

I waited patiently until my name was called and was soon met by a young blond Nazi doctor. The moment he saw me he screamed, "You Polish swine." He sat me forcibly down in a

61

chair and took some blood. He looked at a smear of it under a microscope and told me, "Raus" (out, get lost).

On my way out the door, foolish thoughts crept into my mind. I didn't know if you could tell a Jew from his blood, so I got really worried, though the fact that he threw me out was a good sign, wasn't it? There was so much propaganda in those days that even the Jews were confused.

A few days later, one of the heads of the rail yard, a Herr Chapo came by my billet. He had papers in his hand. He told me that he had said nice things about me to the Gesundheitsamt (Health Directorate) and then leaned over me and said, "Stanislaw, what is it with you, anyway?" I told him that I hadn't any idea what was wrong with the Gesundheitsamt. He then said, "They're all stupid." With that, he put the papers away and that was that!

I had a good friend that I mentioned earlier. His name was Karl Werner and we worked shifts together. Every once in awhile, when there were breaks, Karl would complain about the Jews. Such was the case when we were eating in the big rail restaurant. It was the same night that Hitler's voice came over the radio loud speakers proclaiming that he was uninjured after a failed assassination attempt on him at the Wolf's Lair. Karl and I were talking and he said, "Stanislaw, you are not Polish."

That stunned me and I waited for the other shoe to drop that said, "You are a Jew," but it didn't happen. Instead, Karl, who was not a Nazi, said, "You don't drink. You don't smoke. You can't be Polish!" I laughed, and then he said, "Don't be too free with your words. It's not good." I respected Karl. He was a good and wise man. We worked together for many months, and then the Allied bombing runs started. Railroads were their favorite targets, and we were taking a lot of hits.

Bombed-out barracks in Minden

On one run they clobbered our barracks. Luckily, we weren't in them at the time. I'm sure that many of the cars we loaded, bound for Bremen and other cities never made their destinations.

For me, despite the bombings, the workplace was the safest place to be. I never had arguments with anybody and was careful in my work. I was also careful in my behavior. I never forgot that I was Jewish and where I was, working in the shadow of tyranny.

In Minden, I made friends with non-railroad boys and girls. They worked in factories and other places in the city. I felt more secure and went swimming, played soccer and other games. I was behaving like all the other teenagers. I was now seventeen going on eighteen. During free time, we dressed up and went to the city. Sometimes we took the streetcar to see friends in Porta, but we never wore the letter 'P.' Once, the police stopped us and we had to pay a fine of 20 Marks for not doing so.

In 1943, the really heavy bombardment started. The Allies destroyed a big canal that connected the Weser River and other big rivers in Germany. They hit the railroad and destroyed our barrack as I said. I almost got killed running to the shelter, once. We were very happy to see and hear the bombardment all over Germany. We were sure that the Nazi defeat would come, quickly, though none of us ever dared say so in public. As time passed, many of the people I lived with started talking about the Jews. The filthy Jews. The greedy Jews. The crooked Jews. Some of them spoke with such hatred that I couldn't believe my own ears. One even said that Germany should put up a solid gold monument for killing the Jews. To counter that, a particularly religious person I recall said, "Hitler is an SOB, no good one."

Allied bombs took their toll on Minden

More destruction in Minden

Good friends in Minden in 1943

A musical break with friends in Minden 1944

I had good friend, Josef, a boy like me. He was always good to me, and I felt that we had a solid friendship even though he often spoke badly of the Jews. Once, a fellow worker told me (after the war was over), that had he known I was a Jew he would have informed on me! All were friends with me, as long as my Jewishness was a secret.

One Friday was a particularly rainy and windy day on Ramp Line 16. I saw railroad cars from the city of Bedzin (just northwest of Krakow) that were loaded with Jewish things: bedding, pillows, small tools and household goods, pictures of Jewish families, prayer books and other holy books. There was a breeze and pages were flying all around like so many birds circling. They were landing on the wet road and trucks were rolling over them.

In my mind, those pages being run over were like all of us Jews that were being crushed under the Nazis' boots. I wanted to go and retrieve all of them and give them back to the poor souls with the yellow stars on their coats, but I knew I couldn't. Any compassion for the Jews was regarded as treason. Imagine how I felt. I could not touch anything. My fingers were throbbing and my heart was pounding. I blamed myself for not doing the 'right' thing. Then I forgave myself for staying put and staying alive.

This was just one day, one shift out of many in the world I now inhabited, a world of deception and subterfuge. How I wanted to scream out my real name just once, to hear its sound drift into the sky and to see somebody react to it. Perhaps the sound would carry on the wind to nearby work camps where other Jews could hear it and know that someone outside the barbed wire felt their pain. Once I was given coupons to buy some work clothes for myself. The clothes were in a building separate from the main buildings on the rail yard.

Entering, I saw German women in white uniforms smoking, waiting for customers. One of them took me into a big room. On the floor were piles of used clothing. I suddenly got sick thinking that these clothes once surrounded the bodies of Jews who were now dying in concentration camps or were ashes at the bottom of the ovens of death. I held my hand over my mouth and told her I was sick and needed to leave. I walked out and gulped down a few breaths of air and cleared my lungs, but I could not clear my mind of the clothes and the people who once wore them.

In Minden, one day, I went to a bakery hoping to get some bread. An older woman was behind the counter. I said, "Madam, I am a young person and I work on the railroad and I don't have enough bread. Can you sell me half a loaf?" She responded that she would gladly sell me half a loaf and that I was always welcome to come back if I found myself in the neighborhood again.

On occasion, I needed other services like the time I had trouble with a tooth and went to a an older dentist. I was dressed in a suit, so apparently I made a decent impression, so much so that the man's wife asked me if I had any coffee to give or sell her. I think she thought I was Belgian. Had she known I was a Polish Jew things might have been different. But that day I was just a nice young gentleman in a suit. Her husband fixed my tooth and the filling lasted nearly thirty years!

I was always the youngster in the room, but somehow I impressed the older men with my ability to read and write, and that added a few years on to my perceived age. One of the men asked me to teach one of the other boys the Polish ABCs and to read. This boy and I ultimately became friends.

One day he couldn't help himself and stole a sack of flour and hid it in his locker. Someone must have known about it and informed on him. They arrested him and sent him away to a prison. A few nights later, I heard someone softly whispering, "Stanislaw, can you help me?" The boy had escaped and had come back to our house to beg for assistance. He didn't know where else to go or what else to do. I remembered my own fear all those times I wandered aimlessly in the forest, the terror of being all alone.

We felt sorry for him and we wanted to help, but this simple act of human kindness was fraught with danger. I gave him a shirt and some bread and coffee. Another friend gave him some more clothing. Soon, everybody was there giving him a few Marks to pay for his way back to Poland via Berlin. It was for naught. They caught him on his way out of the compound. He confessed to everything. Soon, they called us to the office. I remember seeing him in the police office with bruises on his face. He was in bad shape. The Gestapo had been called in and had worked their perverse 'magic' on him.

Kazimir and I were called in for interrogation. One by one we went in, were questioned, and came out. When it was my turn, I again felt that sinking feeling in the pit of my stomach and the twin emotions of fear and anger. I was afraid of what they would do to me, and another emotion made me want to just break the boy's bonds and smash the Nazis in the face with them. They asked what part I played in all of this. I told them I had worked at the rail yard for a long time and that I had never been in trouble or had any problems. The police officer told me to wait outside. After a few minutes, the Gestapo man came out and told us, "Tell the truth and I will try to help you." My friend spoke up and said, "Let me answer you, sir, with a question. If this situation were turned around and this was a German boy in there, would you help him?"

71

The Gestapo man thought for a few seconds and said, "Don't do this again. I'll arrange for you all to pay a fine and that will be an end to this." We were grateful for the reprieve and expected that the boy would be released with a fine, too, but they hung him.

We all worked with the daily hope that the war would come to an end soon. The Allied bomb runs were destroying everything. We saw soldiers, airmen, prisoners and civilians walking around in a daze. We felt sorry for them and very close to them, too. There were French and Russian prisoners working on the railroad. Italian prisoners were being guarded by Italian fascist soldiers. Minden was full of foreigners.

Time passed. It was the spring of 1944 in June. I always started out walking to work early because I always stopped to read the war bulletins. This day, I saw something that made my eyes open wide and brought a smile to my mouth. The Allied invasion of Europe had begun! Again, the runner came out and I ran to share the news with my friends. We were sure that this was the beginning of the end for the Germans. We were jubilant and very hopeful that our days at the rail yard were numbered.

Chapter IV
The sunlight of freedom

News came that the Allies had crossed the Rhine River. Liberation was imminent. (Almost another year would pass before we could put down our tools.) It was now April of 1945. Five and a half years had passed since I was forced to leave my boyhood home and my childhood on the doorstep. The Americans and the English were on the other side of the Veyser River. The bridges were destroyed.

Kazimir Rifa was a very intelligent military man and he was also a patient man; he taught me how to swim. He called me "Stasiu." Kazimir was a quiet anti-Semite, and if he had known I was a Jew he probably wouldn't have had anything to do with me. He was always curious about my thoughts and wondered why I didn't open up to him, more.

One day, he said, "We should try to swim the river to escape the Germans." On the way to the river we met a man who said that the SS were close by and that we should be extremely careful. We saw that we could cross under a trestle, but just as we were making our move, an American jeep crossed over and captured us.

Kazimir could speak a little English and managed to convince them that we were not Nazis but were Polish prisoners of the Nazis. The soldiers asked us about hotels and other landmarks in Minden and that's how Kazimir and I spent the first few hours of our liberation, sharing information with the Allied army tank corps whose general, George S. Patton, stood in the distance with his pearl-handled revolver at his side. Years have passed with only the mental image of my family to console me all those times I felt alone or to share my joy at being liberated.

The runner of my youth that had protected me by his speed to flee my captors, had allowed me to use it once again, this time as free men to play sports with boys from different backgrounds - boys that had no idea that underneath the clothing of this soccer-playing teenager lived a Jew.

I would reveal this secret soon as the Americans and the British arrived in Minden in April 1945. We were free, released from the yoke of oppression that had been our home for these many years. We sang and danced and kissed and drank too much and liberated stores of food from German homes. I went into the railroad restaurant and saw that the huge picture of Adolf Hitler was ripped to shreds. We celebrated his demise for two days.

We were unstoppable. We found a cache of schnapps in a basement so we took a chain and attached it to the bars of the cellar window and fixed the other end to a jeep's bumper, and 'boom' the window was open and the booty was ours! Everybody was taking everything. I remember meeting a GI who was an American Indian. He showed us how he could jump and whoop and dance. It was exciting. These were the first few days after which the Americans told us to go easy on the Germans, that the war was behind us now.

The schnapps both dulled our senses and enhanced them. Unfortunately, it also made us do some pretty boneheaded things. We found a machine gun and a lot of bullets. We mounted it on a bicycle and wheeled it around the street and shot it into the air. Soon we saw white flags appearing from windows. That was enough of that. The British quickly restored order. They established a military government and started to take care of all the foreigners. The war was really over! I looked all around and saw no Jewish people, not a one. I decided that it was time for me to share my secret with my friends.

The next morning, I took a long drink and told my best friend (this is the boy who told me he threw rocks at Jews and kicked them) about my secret. His eyes and his whole face changed. "No, Stasiu. This is not possible!" I said, "Juziek, this is true." He said, "You are drunk." He could not believe it. After I told Juziek, I told the others. I got the same reaction from all of them, total disbelief. "This is not possible. This is a joke." I told them it was true and not a joke. The news spread fast. Friends, both boys and girls, came in to ask me the same thing. THIS was liberating, but I needed to reconnect with people of my own faith.

Somebody told me that in the city of Minden lived a German family where the wife was Jewish. The husband bravely saved her from the Nazis. I felt compelled to find the family and did so after searching for a few hours.

I rang the bell and the husband came out. I introduced myself and told him the reason I was there. He asked me to come back in two days, that his wife was sick and he would like to prepare her for the shock of seeing another Jew. He was afraid that she would get too emotional, too excited and that would not be good for her, in her condition. I was happy to oblige and understood, completely.

Two days later, I came back. The man was smiling and very happy to see me. "My wife is waiting for you," he said. I walked into the room. She stretched out her hands crying and beckoned for me to come to her. We started to talk. In the room was a commode and on top of it was a silver candle lighter, a Hebrew prayer book and Bible and other things that were found in Jewish homes. They had prepared all this for me, knowing that these things had been absent from my life for many years. It was a touching reminder of the past and a promise of a future, free from the oppressive regime we had all lived under for so long.

I immediately became a friend of the family. During our conversation, I found out that they had a son almost the same age as me.

After all the celebrations of liberation had faded, I began to realize the reality of my situation. It was then that an enormous sadness set in. Depression followed every time my mind called up memories of all the loved ones I had lost.

The trains were running after liberation and one of my friends went to Hanover. When he returned, he said that there were Jews there so I decided to go, myself. When I arrived, I met many Hungarian Jews, many with their heads shaved. I was dressed well - not fancy mind you but well - and the Jews asked me what I wanted with them.

I told them I was Jewish. "No," they said. "Go to Celle. there is a big camp of displaced persons (DPs) there." I traveled to Celle and looked through the many books containing the names of survivors, hoping I might find some people from Gostynin or Zychlin, a relative, a friend, anybody. I did find the name of a man I knew but he was not in the camp. One person told me that a Rabbi lived in the city and many Jews congregated at his home. I decided to find him.

After a bit of searching, I knocked on the Rabbi's door and walked in. I saw the Rabbi, but behind him I saw my second cousin, Moshe Kelmer. When he saw me he called out, "Yitzi" and he hugged me. Moshe was living in Celle, outside the camp. He told me that he had married a Polish girl, not a Jewish girl, who helped hide him from the Nazis. Forced to live a life in the shadows under an assumed name with someone else's identity and background had been necessary, but now I wanted my own name back. I wanted to once again be Isaac or Yitzak not Stanislaw or Stasiu, Krajcer not Guragczik.

76

It sounds a bit selfish when I say it now. After all, I had survived, and what's in a name when you have been saved from extermination like millions of other human beings? The truth is, our identities are important to all of us.

It's like walking down the only road that can take you home. I had to reclaim my existence, so I went to the nearby office that had been established to take care of displaced persons. As you can imagine, there was a very long line to get in. I saw an British sergeant who spoke German and who had been with Montgomery's 8th Army in Tobruk. I told him that it was essential that I got to speak to the man in charge. He asked, "Warum ist es so wichtig?" *Why is that so important?* I explained that I needed a private meeting.

He took me into an adjacent room and I told him that I was a Jew. He asked if I was really a Jew, and I repeated, "Ich bin Jude. Ich bin Jude" I am a Jew. He smiled and said, "Ich auch." (*Me, too*). THIS was something unexpected. His name was Peter and he was originally from Berlin. It turned out that I was the first Jew he had met since liberation. He was the official interpreter for the office, and I told him that he probably wouldn't meet many more of us for awhile at least.

He listened patiently as I began to recount my experiences after leaving Gostynin. I remember that he often shook his head in disbelief and gave me many reassuring looks. It put me at ease. He asked if I needed food, a place to live, some help. I thanked him, but that the first thing I wanted was my own name back.

He called in an officer, a Major Gray, and summarized my story for him. The officer then took me into his office and asked me many questions. He asked to see my false identification papers.

I handed them over to him, and before my eyes he ripped them to shreds and gave me a new document with my real birth name along with a special letter for the British authorities in case I needed further help.

He told me, "Now you are free, Isaac Krajcer." Free. That was a word I had only dreamt of saying these last five years. I was now a free man. He told me to go and wished me good luck in my new life. I will always remember that kind Englishman for listening to me, and for giving me exactly what I needed to start my new journey, back from the edge of despair.

I would find many new people to help me rebuild my life in DP camps in Celle near Bergen-Belsen, but the first order of business was to bid farewell to the people that made up my small world in Minden...to my friends, the Polish boys and girls. They arranged a goodbye party for me. We hugged and kissed and some cried. We wished each other the best.

My friend Juziek asked me to go with him to Poland. "Stanislaw - I am sorry - Isaac. You are like my brother now. You must come," he said. It hurt me to decline his offer, but he understood. I thanked him, though, from the bottom of my heart. I arrived in Bergen-Belsen in June of 1945, two months after the liberation. A new chapter of my new life was starting. The reality that no one from my family had survived but me had now become a scar where an open wound once was.

I began to put that pain in a special place that all of us have for events too difficult to live with on a daily basis. I searched for weeks for any former resident of Gostynin but found none. The Jews of Gostynin had all perished in what was to become known as the Shoah - the Holocaust.

Bergen Belsen concentration camp

Bergen Belsen barracks

Burning of barracks in Bergen Belsen in May 1945

Chapter V
Hiding in plain sight...again

I needed to feel part of a family, to belong, so I joined a kibbutz and the youth organization that was preparing to go to Palestine. It had been my dream for many years, and at Bergen-Belsen there were many organized Zionist groups just waiting for members. I immediately made new friends and was on my way to healing. We were all adjusting to our new lives. The first holidays of Rosh Hashanah and Yom Kippur I will never forget. On Yom Kippur we said a Yizkor memorial service. The hall was packed with other young survivors from all over.

The Rabbi announced that we would now say the Jewish prayer for the dead, Kaddish, for those souls that have not been found. It was a solemn moment and very profound. Everybody started to cry and some people fainted from the intensity of emotion. The crying went on throughout the service. We were fortunate to be in Bergen-Belsen and lucky, too, that the British were managing it.

My lucky stars were descending from the heavens. I met my future wife, Rachel, there. Rachel was a Holocaust survivor, too. She was lucky that her mother, Rivka, and her twin brother, Aron, had survived. Aron and I quickly became friends. He was also my age and had suffered through three work camps before coming to Bergen-Belsen. After awhile, the 'runner' and I got re-acquainted. There were many activities for us to partake in, like my favorite sport, soccer. Run I did. Everywhere I could. Unlike many of the other people there, I had eaten, regularly, and was in pretty good shape. I remember taking it easy with the others on the field until they got stronger. It would have been unfair for me to use my advantage of steady meals against them.

My soccer team in Bergen Belsen in 1946

Rachel and friends in kibbutz in Bergen Belsen 1946

We all got stronger, day by day. Most of the sick and infirm were healing, gradually, at least their bodies were. For many, however, the trauma of their captivity and brutal treatment was as indelible as the numbers tattooed on their forearms. The new Bergen-Belsen Jewish *community* was rapidly evolving and we got training in various trades.

Organizations were set up. Some families were reunited and everybody was making some sort of plan for the future. That is what people do. They dream. They plan. These things are part of the human condition. They help us drive away the pain and replace it with hope.

My mind was on Palestine. It occupied my waking and sleeping hours. In my kibbutz, there was a man, a Palestinian named Josef Motev (originally Motil) from the Jewish Brigade, from the Haganah. He trusted me and we grew close. He influenced me, greatly, and eventually I joined the organization being one of the first to do so in Bergen-Belsen.

Before I go any further, I must tell you a little more about the Haganah (or Hagana) because it was in this organization that I once again hid in plain sight until I left for Palestine in 1947.

"Although an unofficial underground movement, the Hagana ("defense" in Hebrew) was the primary quasi-military body of the Jewish community in Palestine and the Zionist Movement during the time of the British mandate, prior to the establishment of the State of Israel in 1948.

From that time, the Hagana became the army of the state of Israel – 'Israel Defense Forces' (IDF) (in Hebrew, Tzva Hagana Le-Yisrael – Zahal).

The Hagana was established in 1920 and operated during the next decade under the auspices of the Workers Union ("Histadrut", in Hebrew). Following a period of Arab rioting, in August 1929, the Hagana became the "official", though secret, military wing of the Zionist Jewish Agency and the National Jewish Committee (Vaad Leumi) of Palestine. The Hagana General Command comprised six public representatives from the left and center-right Jewish parties.

The main assignment of Hagana was to provide security to Jewish life and property against Arab violence, which had caused the deaths of more than 700 Jews between 1920 and 1939.

Growing from a modest beginning of a few thousand, the Hagana soon became a large, well-organized quasi-military body of tens of thousands of men and women. The British Government regarded the Hagana as an illegal underground organization, but for the Jewish population, it constituted a vital source of defense and security. Under the elected national institutions, it soon became the armed forces of the State in the making.

Up until 1939, the Hagana focused on static protection of settlements, towns and other communities in pre-State Israel (called "Palestine"), based on the principle of defensive operations, building up and training military forces, as well as striving to acquire arms from every possible source, including clandestine manufacturing of weapons.

After the bloody Arab uprising of 1936 to 1939, the Hagana changed its strategy from defending from "within the fences" to offensive operations outside the domain of Jewish settlements and developed a mobile warfare doctrine.

During that period, the first offensive units were established: first the mobile unit (Nodedet), then the field companies (Fosh) , and the famous "Special Night Squads" (SNS) under the command of a pro-Zionist Scottish Officer, Orde Charles Wingate. Those offensive operations, carried out day and night, had a tremendous effect in reducing the attacks of the Arab bands and helped the British Mandatory Government to suppress the uprising.

In the spring of 1939, a severe crisis developed after the British Government had changed the policy it had pursued since the Balfour Declaration (1917), issuing what was termed a "White Paper", recommending a series of pro-Arab steps and legislation, such as curtailing Jewish immigration and placing restrictions on purchase of land and on the establishment of new settlements by Jews. The Hagana was in the process of planning an armed confrontation against the British authorities, but withheld this program with the outbreak of World War II in the fall of 1939.

During the war, the Hagana assisted the British in many ways, including Intelligence, and sent parachutists into German-occupied countries in Europe. About 30,000 Palestinian Jews (men and women), most of them members of the Hagana, joined the British Armed Forces in the war against Nazi Germany. In fact, the entire Jewish population, less than half a million, was mobilized to participate in the war effort.

As of 1939, the Hagana was re-organized and General Headquarters were formed led by the Chief of the General Staff (to be continued when the Hagana became Israel's Defense Forces in 1948). Besides helping the British in the war against Nazi Germany, the Hagana strengthened and improved its military capability.

Thousands of youngsters aged 18-25 were organized and trained within the framework of "Field-Corps" (Chish) and "Home-guards" (Chim) to protect cities, towns and settlements. "Youth Battalions" (Gadna) were formed in which teenagers, both boys and girls, acquired pre-military training enabling them to join the ranks of the Hagana.

Services such as intelligence, a signals corps, medical corps, and small air and maritime units were founded. Clandestine factories started to manufacture small arms, mortars and ammunition. Thousands, sent by the Hagana, served in the British Police units, mainly as the Jewish Settlements Police. The highlight was the establishment of the "Palmach" (Hebrew abbreviation of striking force) – the only fully mobilized force – created in 1941. The Palmach grew within four years from six companies to four battalions, soon to be organized as a brigade, directly under the command of the Hagana General Staff.

The Palmach units, consisting of young men and women, were stationed in kibbutzim, where they underwent advanced military training but also worked in order to support themselves, while also scouting the country and getting to know every corner of it. Following the end of World War II, the Palmach led the struggle against the hostile British forces until they evacuated the country at the end of the British mandate in Palestine in May 1948. Throughout the War of Independence, especially in its initial stages, the Palmach constituted the major fighting force against Arab assaults and invasions. The need to operate secretly, with only the most meager means and inadequate arms and other facilities, promoted a unique type of strategic military thinking, guerilla tactics and battlefield ethics that involved pioneering spirit, leadership in battle, high motivation, originality in planning, taking initiative and resourcefulness.

The Hagana was based not merely on a hierarchy of ranks but on mutual understanding, equality of rights and duties, friendship, devotion to the cause and to each other.

The notion was that when necessary, every soldier is capable to function as a commander (a Palmach slogan "every squad leader – a general"). As noted earlier, in 1939, the Hagana was re-structured, setting up a professional General Staff, headed by the Chief of Staff. This concept was later installed in the IDF, and remains until today.

In addition to building up a military force and preparing the Jewish population for the future challenges, the Hagana took on two other important tasks at the very core of the Zionist mission -- to maintain the continued immigration (Aliya) of Jews into Palestine by any means and to assure the secured establishment of new Jewish settlements.

Thus, from 1936 to the end of the British mandate in 1948, the Hagana initiated and participated in setting up about 140 new settlements, some of which were known as "tower and stockade". Eleven of these were put up in the Negev in the course of a single night in October of 1946. It may well be said that these settlements actually determined the borders of the new State in the making.

Once the British adopted a policy of restricting Jewish immigration into Palestine (following the publication of the "White Paper", and even before), the Jewish national institutions found ways and means to clandestinely bring in Jews under cover, by land and sea. This so-called "illegal immigration" (Ha'apala) began even before World War II, but it was in the forties that the Hagana took upon itself the responsibility of bringing in tens of thousands of Jewish immigrants who had survived the Holocaust.

During this same period, Jews from North Africa and Middle Eastern countries also reached a safe harbor in Palestine.

Over 120,000 Jews were brought in by more than 100 ships – acquired, equipped, navigated and commanded by a handful of Palmach youngsters. In the early 1930s, a few hundred members left the Hagana and formed a right-wing military body, called "Irgun B". In 1937, most of them re-joined the ranks of the Hagana, while the rest formed the "Etzel" (Irgun Zevai Leumi), which in turn split into "Lehi" (Lohamei Herut Israel), both small right-wing nationalist groups with an extremist ideology with regard to the struggle against the Arabs and the British. Neither of these two groups accepted the authority of the national Jewish Authorities.

Towards the end of the war and after, the Hagana intensified its struggle – by political and even violent acts against British rule, along with more illegal immigration and further unauthorized settlements, in response to Britain's opposition to the creation of an independent Jewish state (Ben-Gurion: "We will fight the Germans as if there is no White Paper, and the British as if there is no war with the Germany").

For a period of some nine months, the "Hagana," "Etzel", and "Lehi" acted in concert (the "Hebrew Resistance Movement"), though independently, against the British, led by the Hagana. The three organizations informed each other before carrying out their operations. During this time, the Hagana performed many courageous acts, including raids on British police stations and destruction of British Radar installations. In the course of one night, they blew up 12 bridges disconnecting Palestine from the neighboring Arab countries, freed hundreds of immigrants captured by the British and held as prisoners in the Atlit camp, and caused serious damage to the mandatory railway lines and more.

In all these operations, the Hagana took care as far as possible to avoid causing civilian casualties

The cooperation among the Jewish military resistance groups came to an end in July 1946 when, without authorization of the national Jewish authorities, the Etzel blew up the King David Hotel in Jerusalem – killing many civilians, Jews, Arabs, and Englishmen. The operations against the British continued. The Hagana focused mainly on accelerating illegal immigration, attacking British ships and radar installations used to stop immigrants from entering the country; and setting up new settlements in border areas.

In addition, major effort was devoted to building a strong military force, based on the Palmach and Chish, in order to prepare for what was considered an imminent war against the Arabs over control of Palestine. More undercover arms factories were constructed, weapons were acquired abroad, and young Holocaust survivors were trained in Europe and at the detention camps in Cyprus.

From the summer of 1947, the "Hagana" intensified preparations for a large-scale war against the local Arab militias and the armies of the Arab states. By the time it had become clear that the British were about to leave Palestine and that a war would soon break out, David Ben Gurion assumed responsibility for matters of defense. The Hagana was then organized to include the Palmach brigade, five infantry brigades, and other military services. Veterans of the British Army were also integrated into this general force, contributing their fighting skill and experience.

War broke out in December 1947, immediately after the U.N. resolution about the partition of Palestine and the establishment of a Jewish state.

The Hagana became the fighting force that defended the Jewish population in Palestine until the declaration of the State of Israel in May 1948, and continued as such until becoming the Israel Defense Force.

During the first six months of heavy fighting, the Hagana managed to mobilize, equip, train, and activate a military power of about 50,000 men and women, functioning in 12 brigades, a nuclei of air and naval forces, alongside other units and services that exist in modern armies. During this period the Hagana forces broke the backbone of the Arab offensive and conquered strategic territories to resist the invasion of the armies of five Arab states. Up to May 1948, the Hagana forces finally succeeded in repelling most of the invading armies; and on June 1st, the Hagana became the Israel Defense Forces.

The last Hagana Chief of Staff, General Yaakov Dori, took over as the first Chief of Staff of the IDF. The Hagana brigades became IDF brigades and its air and naval services became the Israeli Air Force and Navy, with all the other units and services being similarly transformed. David Ben-Gurion, the first Prime Minister of the State of Israel, described the importance of the Hagana in a famous speech on the day when the IDF was sworn in: "Without the experience, the planning, the operational abilities, the commanding officers, the loyalty and the courage of the Hagana, the Jewish community could not have withstood the terrible bloody battles, and we never would have seen the rise of the State of Israel. In the history of the Jewish people the chapter of the Hagana will shine in glory and grandeur forever".

The preceding was gratefully reprinted from the History of the Hagana (www.irgon-hagana.co)

It took quite awhile for Jews in Europe to become reunited, to find what was left of their families and to dedicate themselves to the future. Being future-oriented was not something European Jews had done for five long years at least, and the decimation of our people during those years made it an uphill struggle to achieve even a small semblance of optimism. What did motivate many of us was our dream of coming to Palestine and making it a Jewish homeland free from oppression.

I shared this dream and that's why I joined the Haganah, to help facilitate a pathway out of Germany for Jews to Palestine. The Haganah's mission in Germany was one of spiriting mostly young Jewish men out of the country using false papers to Palestine as the British had imposed rigid visa restrictions (15,000 per year for five years and then zero). Legal immigration was called, *Aliyah Aleph* and *Haganah* means defense.

If the Haganah hadn't already existed, someone would have created it because European Jews were homeless and needed resettling. Their villages were destroyed and their homes were given over to non-Jews who weren't interested in having them return to challenge ownership.

The establishment of the groundwork for creating the State of Israel was moving fast, and at the end of 1946 Nahum Goldmann (a leading Zionist and founder of the World Jewish congress) was working feverishly to get an agreement on restitution and rehabilitation for the remaining Jews in Germany. Goldmann was an ardent believer in a two-state solution for Palestine and was a tireless advocate for allowing the best and brightest of European Jewry to the emerging state.

I shared Goldmann's beliefs, and in 1946 I was called by my friend Josef Motev of the Haganah to make the transfer of Jews through the DP camps like Bergen-Belsen to Palestine a reality. This was a life-saving mission for many Jews who yearned for freedom, and I was proud to help make it happen. The Haganah had two principal escape routes: the northern route was through Berlin and the southern was through Munich.

Bricha helped smuggle Jews to Palestine

Me at Bricha's Hanover HQ in 1945

Our Berlin Bricha gang in 1946

My first assignment was to go to Aachen near the Belgian border to do some reconnaissance. I found out that it was a nest of black marketeering. I came back and made my report. After that, I was asked to go to Dusseldorf and find a special man, a Haganah man, who was working with the military. I was to bring an empty suitcase full of blank passports back to Bergen Belsen where they would be forged and given to young Jewish men who were headed for Palestine.

I should say at this point that extraordinary circumstances often require extraordinary risks. If I had been found out, I would have certainly been jailed. Such were the risks many of us took to populate the Jewish state with patriots.

(I also 'shepherded' small groups of men from Hannover to Belgium, twice. I trained them before we left so that we would not encounter and trouble.)

After picking up the passports in Dusseldorf, I headed for the train station, fully aware that spot checks were conducted on luggage (the authorities were looking for contraband, counterfeit money, and falsified travel documents, etc.). The trip went well, the suitcase was stashed above the seats opposite me on the other side of the aisle (to give me plausible deniability in case it was discovered).

Everything went smoothly. I returned via Hanover to Celle to Bergen-Belsen. Mission was completed. The next steps were to get the young men dressed in uniforms, have their photos taken and then turn the passports over to the forgers. I did this a couple of times. Next, they sent me to Greiffenberg (which is near Stettin) with a load of black market items that I would use as bribes to local officials. (I might add that the Haganah was not actively engaged in the black market trade.)

The day after my arrival, it was a Sunday, I knocked on the door of the private residence of the Burgermeister (mayor). After introductions and some small talk, I asked him what he proposed to do about all the German Jews (some were Polish Jews) coming through his town from the East.

He asked what was expected or needed of him. I told him that we wanted to use Greiffenberg as a transit point for these Jews. The first stop to bring in people from Poland was usually Berlin. From there they could get to Hanover, then Celle, then Bergen-Belsen. The Burgermeister was willing to assist us (he had helped Jews before) and took my colleague and I around to several properties where people in transit could stay, unnoticed. One property was a large farm capable of hosting hundreds. We agreed on using it. To cement the deal I gave him most of the black market items I had been carrying. His cooperation became crucial to our success.

The Burgermeister also fixed me up with lodging for the night and the next morning he and I visited the local police station where I extracted promises from 5-6 police to look the other way when necessary. Since the police chief lived across the street from where I was staying, I took a chance and invited him over. He came and I introduced myself, referred to my meeting with the Burgermeister and soon we discussing the details of our request of him.

He was very amenable and told me of his pregnant wife, the cost of living on a police chief's salary, etc. I commiserated with him and asked what he was being paid. When he told me, I said that we would double that amount in exchange for his help whenever we needed it. He asked what kind of help we needed. I told him that at some point the Russians would be asking him questions about any possible people illegally transiting Greiffenberg.

All I wanted was for him to tell me when those questions were asked and by whom. He agreed and I gave him the rest of the items in my suitcase, food, mostly. Another mission accomplished. It made me feel good to be useful to the Haganah and to help pave the way for our 'exports' to Palestine. Soon, Jewish refugees were streaming through Greiffenberg. Our boys were wearing Russian uniforms and transported in Russian trucks. So heavy was the weight, the ground was literally shaking when they made their way to the farm. They quickly unloaded their cargo and left to grab another load of men. And so it continued.

One time, trucks carrying 110 children came and the Russians were getting suspicious so I secreted the children away in an inconspicuous place in the farm and told the woman to watch over them and cover them with hay, if necessary. The Russians searched the farm but found nothing and went away satisfied that they had done their job.

I went straight to the police chief and asked what on earth was happening, why I hadn't been warned. He calmed me down and told me that this was routine and the Russians were just 'checking the boxes.' One evening a few days later in Greiffenberg I got a phone call from the Haganah in Berlin telling me to stay put. A little later I heard banging on my window. It was two boys. Right away I told them to come in.

They said they wanted out of Germany and I told them I would take them with me to the train station the next morning. I would buy them tickets for Berlin. The next morning we navigated our way through the police at the station (they all knew me by now) and the two youngsters board their train. I got word that they arrived safely and that the Haganah was pleased. From that moment on, I was taking people from Berlin to Bergen-Belsen fairly routinely.

Things didn't always go as planned. One time I 'lost' a whole group of people. It happened like this...I told the group to always keep their eyes on me as I couldn't be seen as the leader of their group; I needed to keep a safe distance from them. They lost eye contact and we were separated. It happened when we descended some steps on one train platform in order to go up some steps on the adjacent one.

I saw them, thank God, and motioned for them to join me. The train for Magdeburg was getting ready to pull out. Fortunately for us there was a delay because the Station Master had to put on an additional car because the train was so full. This gave them enough time to board the new car. All were safely on board and I breathed a sigh of relief.

There was also some time for leisure amid my Haganah missions. In March/April 1946 there was big athletic meet in the British sector of Germany which included running and soccer. I had trained for it all through the winter, and when the time came for the meet I was lucky enough to win a trophy for my performance.

I was so proud. As a matter of fact, I carried it with me to the U.S. when Rachel and I emigrated, but at a point I felt that this was something that belonged in the Holocaust Museum in Washington, D.C. so I donated it to them. Back to the Haganah. Life went on and I went back to my work for the Haganah. I remember somebody was supposed to give me advice as to how to cross the border in Berlin to the Russian side. I took two girls with me (The Haganah had given me 200 marks to help them). I never crossed a border before. At the station, I met a young man and we talked. I asked him if he was going to cross the border. He said, "yes." I then pointed to the girls and asked if we could all go, together (I gave him some cigarettes). It was getting dark and he said, "Sit down with me."

A little later we heard screaming and shooting! He said, "Don't worry." We waited some more and then we crossed on foot.

We separated from him at Magdeburg. Myself and the two girls saw many Russian soldiers, but nobody bothered us. Maybe because it was so late and they were tired, I don't know. We took the train to Berlin and arrived in the night. Berlin was a bombed-out but huge city. It was a hot humid night and we went to a part of Berlin called, Wittenau. I delivered the girls to the Haganah. One girl ended up getting a job managing money with the Bricha (another Jewish organization - *Bricha* means *escape*) and the other one got a job preparing food in the kitchen. I became very familiar with the layout of the city and more aware of how to avoid the Russians.

As I think back, I was either very bold or very reckless to take the chances I took. I had travel and ID documents in English and in Hebrew (which the Russians couldn't read) and I showed them to whomever questioned me, whenever the occasion arose. I made friends with the heads of the train stations and told them I was formerly one of them - a railroad worker - and I could speak the lingo. Whenever I needed large numbers of tickets I would rap on the back door of the ticket master and tell him how many and I got them, no questions asked. I know my superiors thought me bold, and I will settle for that.

At the end of 1946 beginning of 1947 the head of the World Jewish Agency, Nahum Goldmann visited us. He came to our place (quite illegally) in Berlin in Wittenau and he gave us a nice talk. He knew very well how dangerous our missions were, especially with the Russians all around.

Goldmann said that if any of us wanted to go to Palestine from Bergen Belsen with the first transport of 400 people, we could go. This sounded good to me. I was ready to take the final step to a new home in Palestine. Myself and three others went across the border and made our way to Bergen Belsen.

I told Rachel and her mother that we were all going to get to go to Palestine and we got our papers/permits prepared by the Jewish agency, Hayas, in coordination with the kibbutz. We then began to bid our friends, farewell. It was bittersweet, leaving, but we were so excited that worry had to wait. We were taken by train to a transit camp in Nord Westphalica. Then we all boarded a train bound for Marseilles by way of Minden.

I knew we had to change engines in Minden, so I thought it would be a good idea to see if any of the 'old gang' of railroaders was there. To my surprise they certainly were, and I was greeted like a conquering hero. We embraced each other and I promised to write to them. The train pulled out and I found myself waving to anyone who would notice like departing tourists generally do. I also remember feeling that a part of me was left on that platform watching the train depart. My thoughts at the time were of my parents and brothers and others that I had lost, but they were also of my new soul mate, Rachel Straser. Who would have guessed that I would have found her at a German prison camp, in this place where so many souls were lost?

No renaissance painter could have captured her beauty in the way I saw it through my eyes. She was stunning with long black hair and a face that spoke sweetly to a young man...and she was sitting right beside me on this train! I am sure that many of the same thoughts went through Rachel's mind: about her brothers and her father...and about the new challenge she was facing.

103

She may have been quiet during the trip, but I later found out that her stillness is born of an abiding inner peace. As a matter of fact, everyone wanted to be around her. She projected back on people their best as she did with me. That is one of the reasons we fell in love and why we have been together as man and wife for over 70 years. As you will read, later, we were married in Palestine on October 28, 1947. I am sure that my mother was looking down, smiling on us as we took our vows, and saying to herself, "He's all grown up now. Finally, he's done with all this running!"

Chapter VI
A new home beckons

I had never been to Marseilles. Neither had I ever crossed an ocean on a ship named 'Providence', nor had I done so with a beautiful girl at my side. Rachel, Rachel's mother and I alighted our land transportation and boarded the ship, 'Providence.' What a fitting name! We all filed down to the bottom of the ship where there were bunks set up and tables and chairs. Since this was the first day of Passover, all of us Jews were in a jubilant and festive mood. We were pilgrims, leaving the known, heading towards the unknown from the bottom of a ship in steerage. I think if you had asked any of us that day if it bothered us to sail 'economy class' we would have probably looked at you in wonderment for even asking the question.

In addition to being Jewish, we were survivors of the greatest purge of humanity ever known. We would forever be mourning the loss of our families and loved ones and were leaving the countries of our birth - in my case, my Polish homeland and the sights, smells, and sounds of Gostynin and Zychlin.

Before departing Europe I had written a letter to my mother's cousin, Isaac Kelmer. I told him that we would arriving the last day of Passover and that I was looking forward to meeting him. (He had left Poland in the early 1920s to migrate to Palestine.) Our destination was the Palestinian port of Haifa. Rachel and I were filled with energy and enthusiasm and hope... and a bit of trepidation. We sighted Haifa and it seemed to take forever to sail those last few miles, but the ship docked to a roar of cheers from all on board. Rachel and her mother would go to Rachel's aunt's house and I would go to the Kelmers'.

I was one of the first to disembark and down the gangplank I scurried, carrying my backpack. Suddenly, I heard my name called. It was a colleague from the Haganah in Frankfurt! He asked me if he could help me in any way, but I said that I had everything under control. He countered with, "Just as I suspected. You are running true to form. At least let me give you transportation," and he called over a man on a motorcycle with a sidecar. I hopped in and away we flew to my uncle's building.

The driver rang the bell while I collected my things and straightened my clothes and my uncle came to the door. "Oh, you are Yitzak!" He invited me in and on the table lay fresh oranges, cake, wine. I couldn't believe my eyes. What beautiful fruit and such a wonderful flat! This uncle was my grandmother's brother and his wife was my mother's friend (my grandmother had many children). Many people were crammed into the house and they were all embracing me and asking what had become of my family. They gave me the key to the house and said, "This is your home for as long as you like." I was moved to tears by their kindness and generosity.

This was truly the first day of the rest of my life and I was taking it all in, recording every detail in my mind.

~

Gradually the present took the place of the past, and I began a number of new routines. I saw Rachel nearly every day and our romance and friendship blossomed. I joined a soccer club and got my running legs back in shape. It wasn't long after that the coach told me that I belonged on their first team as I was, obviously, an experienced player. Some of other players, one young man in particular, was a bit jealous and he purposely tripped me and I was injured for awhile.

Nothing too serious, just painful and irritating because it meant I couldn't play. It was after seven weeks with the Kelmers that I got restless. I was now 22 years old and felt like a pioneer, having left my homeland and was now where I wanted to be, in Palestine, at the dawn of the birth of a new country. I talked it over with Rachel and we both felt that we needed a new start, away for ourselves, and in another part of Palestine.

My friends from the Bricha brigade were organizing a new group that would leave Haifa and move inland to the country and they asked Rachel and I to join them. THIS was what I was waiting for. We agreed and we both we taken to a kind of preparatory camp where would learned about agriculture and animal husbandry. We had a vegetable garden and I worked on the irrigation system and on some farm implements like tractors and such.

Across from us was a beautiful Moshav (a famers' collective) where everybody lived separately but worked together sharing the heavy farm equipment. It was a different life from smuggling human beings to safety, that's for sure. I felt proud and happy. I had realized a dream. There was all sorts of work to be done in these final months of 1947.

I remember once I was given a big gun and told to stand guard around the water pipes as there was occasional sabotage. It was very early in the morning when I heard a click, click, click. In the dim light I could see a donkey and a man dressed in Arab clothing sitting on it. The man appeared to be friendly. He said something to me like salam, salam, but not speaking Arabic or even Hebrew for that matter, I didn't understand him and was afraid that he meant me harm. I showed him the gun and told him to 'get lost'! He raised his stick and waved it in the air. Who could blame him?

On the kibbutz in 1949

Soon, I learned a few words of Hebrew and Arabic so that I could challenge someone without insulting or agitating them. Soon, too, my group was ready to go out on our own. We went to a settlement in the lower Galilee where they needed more people. It was a settlement with 60 cows and 250 sheep and horses and mules, tractors and good growing land. We all had small houses, one room and a kitchen.

Farming was our way of life. Unfortunately, I grew a bit impatient over time. I expected the other settlers to treat me equally, but I felt a little like a second-class citizen. There were the older locally-born citizens and then there was us, the foreign-born European immigrants. It's difficult to explain, but the feeling persisted.

Trouble was brewing among the Arabs, so everywhere became the front lines for the Jewish population. We were always on our guard. Plenty of fences were constructed. There were many bright spots in our lives, however. The first was my marriage to Rachel on October 27, 1947. Another came in November of 1948 with the birth of our first son, Jona (John) named after Rachel's father. Because of the rainy season, Rachel had to go to the hospital three weeks early so that we were certain she could be admitted before the roads became impassable.

During the rainy season the only way to leave the settlement was on a donkey or by tractor, and very few women would have chosen either one. Unfortunately, the Arab/Israeli war broke out in 1948 and nearly half the population of each settlement was told to be ready to fight as there was no standing army in Israel. Our settlement was heavily guarded at night and an escape vehicle was always standing by during the day to get the women and children to safety.

Rachel and Jona in the kibbutz 1949

To some, it may seem strange that I willingly jumped from the 'frying pan' of post-war Europe to the 'fire' of Israel's conflict. I never questioned myself about my decision when I thought back to the many years - since my early boyhood in the Zionist organizations - where Palestine was my dream. There is strife in every life, but that doesn't mean that we should give up when adversity smacks us in the face! I thanked God that I had my life, a family, and was living out my dream in a place that felt like home. We were not well off by any means without parents to help us during the early years of our marriage as many of the local citizens had. We struggled.

A year later, in 1950, we started to seriously think about leaving. We did leave the settlement and moved to Haifa and I got a job on the railroad. We lived with Rachel's mother for a time, but a friend of mine from Bricha who I knew in Germany helped us get our own apartment soon thereafter. The Israeli railroad was a pretty antiquated system and not the kind of place that offered any kind of future for me but it was a job I knew.

The yardmaster saw that I was an industrious worker and he encouraged me to take a few hours of Hebrew language training each week which I did. I remember one night we arranged the off-loading of a 20-car train very quickly. The next morning the yardmaster called me in and asked how in Heaven's name I could do that. I simply said, "That is my job; that is what I do, today and every day." He was so impressed that he gave me a promotion, an assistant yardmastership.

In the meantime, I was called up for military service for 18 months. I went for some schooling and when I was done they put me in charge of a platoon because of my prior experience with the Haganah. I received machine gun and logistical field training with map-reading.

I finished my service but not before contracting typhus and spent time in a military hospital before I went back to the railroad.

A few years later, in 1954, our daughter, Zahava was born. We were overjoyed, but two years after that something happened to her. She couldn't breathe properly and the doctors were mystified; they couldn't explain it. One evening I came home and the door was unlocked and nobody was there. I ran to the doctor thinking that's where my family was, and the doctor told me that she had admitted Zahava to the hospital. When I got there I saw her in an oxygen tent. She looked so fragile and helpless with a bluish cast to her face. Her breathing was labored.

They took plenty of tests for allergies. Nothing. No allergies. The doctor was concerned for her little heart, that it couldn't take the stress. A specialist, a pediatrician, originally from Czechoslovakia, was called in. After examining her he told us, "This place is not for her. Try to cross the ocean to America. You might save her." I was shocked at her condition and equally shocked at the prospect that to save our daughter we would have to uproot ourselves and move again, this time to a country where Jews were a definite minority.

After discussing this possibility with my brother-in-law, Aron, who was living in Massachusetts, I came to the conclusion that it was the only right thing to do for Zahava. We would have to plan for an eventual move. Then, the 1956 war broke out and I was called up as a reservist, instructing the new troops. My company commander told me that this conflict was very real and very different from the 1948 war. I was taken near the Syrian border on a dangerous mission in a kind of no-man's land, but came back unhurt. A few other encounters later and the war was over for me.

112

It was now 1958 and our plans to leave Israel were firmed up.

We were all set to leave but not before we were interviewed at the U.S. Consulate. I was there with my ten year old son. The Vice-Consul asked him, "Are you a Communist?" He turned to me and said, "Papa, what is a Communist?" I was barely able to suppress a laugh and neither was the Vice-Consul. We then drove to the airport where Rachel and Zahava were waiting. Again, we bade farewell to yet another homeland with the same kind of mixed feelings we had leaving Europe. Something wonderful happened on board that plane a half-hour into the flight. Suddenly, and without warning, our daughter started breathing normally, again. We couldn't believe our eyes. She was crawling around on the floor. It was a miracle!

Chapter VII
Welcome to the USA

The time for leaving Israel was rapidly approaching. Not only were we mentally prepared for our big move to the United States, but we scraped together enough money from the sale of our house to buy airplane tickets for a family of four. KLM Royal Dutch Airlines would carry us across the ocean to the new world (for us anyway) of the United States. I remember my head being full of many thoughts as we boarded the plane. How would we manage in a new country without speaking English? Would we be welcome there.

How did the Americans treat Jews from Israel? What kind of work could I find to provide for my family. Would Zahava's medical condition improve (she wasn't feeling well when we took off)? Well, we needn't have worried about it because within a half hour after takeoff she was breathing normally and playing about like a normal child on the floor! It was, as I may have said before, a miracle!

This was also my first time flying in such a big plane. Such comfortable seats and refreshments. We felt like privileged people on an exciting expedition traveling at 500 miles an hour to a new future! I wish I could say that we were financially secure, but I can't. All I had in my pocket was the rest of our savings, $700. Who knew how long that would last us? I sure didn't. Fortunately, we were to be met by my brother-in-law, Aron, at Kennedy Airport so we felt somewhat secure.

After clearing customs we all went out into this massive space. We looked around for Aron, but he was nowhere to be seen, so we waited, and waited.

I wanted to ask somebody how we could page him , maybe, but I realized that I couldn't find the English words to do that. Fortunately, one of the officers on the plane asked if he could help us (in German). Gratefully, I spoke to him and told him we were sort of, stranded there. My brother-in-law was not there. He told me not to worry that he would help me. We wouldn't be sleeping in the streets of New York. "Just wait here," he said.

He came back and said, "Do you have a telephone number you can call?" I said, "Yes, I have the number of my grandmother's sister." He then called the number and got her on the phone. She told him to put all of us a taxi and gave him the address. "Send them to us," she said. We piled into a taxi with all our luggage and arrived at their apartment in Brooklyn. I immediately called Judy, Aron's wife and asked if Aron had forgotten us. She apologized and said that they got the date wrong and that Aron would come by to pick us up the following day.

We all slept soundly that night, tired from our long journey. The next day we were on our way to Dorchester, just outside of Boston. We stayed at the home of my mother-in-law that night. I remember being uneasy, not speaking any English, walking around in a daze. While there I found a man who asked me if I wanted to work. I was not going to refuse the opportunity to work, so I accepted and he took me to his butcher shop and gave me an apron. I was to sweep up and do cleaning of the shop.

Rachel was concerned about Zahava and took her to the children's hospital, Beth Israel, to have her checked. The abrupt turnaround in her health on the plane was wonderful, but we wanted to make sure that she was alright. The doctors examined her and told us that she was fine and that she would only get better.

What wonderful news this was! From that moment on, whenever I was a little sad or maybe disappointed, I thought of my wonderful daughter and her blossoming health.

I soon quit the job and went to apply for work in Everett at a sweater factory. I got the job and met many wonderful people there. It seems that I worked too fast, and the shop steward asked me if I would join the union. I joined, and after a few weeks, I'm giving you a different job, that of a cutter.

I was cutting patterns, and after a few months I was in Boston and met a person who asked me if I wanted to work as a barber in a hospital (he had a concession to provide barbering services to hospitals) and when I was finished giving shaves and haircuts there I could come to his barber shop and work there.

I needed to have a license to cut hair, so I took an examination and passed with flying colors. It really wasn't much of an achievement as I had been cutting hair since I was a teenager in Poland, but I was proud that I did. A Master's license was my ticket to a better job. The hospital/barber shop job wasn't very satisfying, but it was work, but I was ambitious. As a new immigrant, I was occasionally taken advantage of when it came to leases on apartments. I ended up paying for things that I shouldn't have paid for, but I learned, quickly. We were living in Dorchester at the time. My family was settling in. Jona joined the scouts and we were becoming Americans. little by little.

My language skills improved largely because I went to night school. Soon we were all speaking English and making friends. It reminded me of my days learning German and seeing how important language was to being accepted and moving up in the world.

Our home in Newton in 1969

Lenny and I in Newton

John, Lenny and Zahava in 1960

Rachel, Zahava and Lenny in 1960

Life was good, and slowly the memories of all the bad times during the war were receding into the background.

One day while reading the paper I saw an advertisement. The owner of a barber shop in Newton, Massachusetts was looking for another barber. I made the trip and met the owner who was a very friendly man, Al Sadler, in his seventies. He, too, was an immigrant, a German who had come to the U.S. just prior to the First world War. We hit it off, well, and he said, "Please stay here and work for me." I told him that I had to give notice to my present employer, so he said, "Just tell them you are going on vacation and leave!" Reluctantly, I did what he said, but my employer was cross with me. I was a good worker and he didn't want to lose me.

Working in Newton, at this shop, was the best thing that could have happened to me. I found someone who understood me, was happy for me and treated me like his son, and he paid me well. I soon got the nickname, 'Ike.' Why I don't know, but I became Ike (again with another name like Stanislaw!). I treated him as well as he treated me.

I cleaned around his chair, picked up his things when I saw that it pained him to do so. We respected and liked each other. Ours was more a friendship than a pure employer/employee relationship. Every day, when I got up in the morning, I looked forward to standing on that barber shop floor for eight hours.

There came a time when, in the early 60s, we were talking with one another about the future and he said, "Why don't you buy half of my shop? You have a family to think of and my family is grown and doesn't need me so much, anymore." We agreed, and so Yitzak, the runner, the trainman had now become half-owner of his own barbering business.

It would have made my parents proud. We modernized the shop and added a third chair and business was good until one day my partner had a stroke and collapsed. He was rushed to the hospital but never recovered. His widow, who was a very generous and caring person, asked if I wanted to buy his share of the shop. I said, "Yes, I would be honored to do so."

I was now the sole owner of the Center Barber Shop in Newton. I knew that I needed to negotiate a long-term lease on the shop with the Irish owner. He was a very reasonable and friendly man and gave me good terms. I built up the business over the years and had a steady clientele of many well-known and highly respected men. Not every man was a gentleman, though.

There were times when I heard customers make anti-Semitic statements (they didn't know I was a Jew) and it took me back to the days in my childhood when the word, 'Zyd,' was thrown around. I steeled myself when these kinds of comments were made and forced a smile to my face. Fortunately, these incidents were few and far between, but they hurt, nonetheless.

We belonged to the Temple Beth El which was a modern orthodox temple, and I always prayed for people who were prejudiced, knowing that nothing I could do could change their attitudes. Maybe God would have a better chance at it. I was always working on Saturday (it was the shop's busiest day). I explained it to the Rabbi and he completely understood.

They say that nothing succeeds like success, and my shop radiated success. It was always full of customers. As it would happen, one day many years later, I put an ad in the paper.

My barber shop in Newton, MA

"For sale, a successful barber shop in Newton." I was testing the water, and soon after the ad appeared, a man came by the shop and asked me, "Ike, what do you want for the shop?" I didn't really have a figure in mind, but I said, "$20,000." To my surprise, he said, "Alright." He went home, wrote out a check and came back, and that was that. The Center Barber Shop changed hands.

Part of our deal was that I would work a little while in the shop to make a smooth transition so that he wouldn't lose any customers because of my departure. The new owner kept in touch with me over the years and he told me that that shop helped put his three children through college. What a wonderful thing to think that my old shop would finance the education of three young people just as it helped my family over those many years.

I retired from the shop but not from life. I joined many different organizations and participated in community events as well as played golf and tennis (I played tennis up until last year when it became too much of a strain on my joints).

After awhile, the warmth of Florida beckoned and we made an exploratory trip there; Rachel and I liked it in Century City and pretty soon we decided to move for good. It was 1998 and we said goodbye to New England, our first American home, but began a new and wonderful chapter in our lives.

At this point I must say a few words about my new adopted country, the United States. There are many people who take its freedoms for granted, but not me and certainly not survivors of the Holocaust. Each day in America is a blessing, and I have been so lucky to have been able to make a living here, see my children grow up in a place of great opportunity and to make so many wonderful friends. God bless this great country!

Rachel and I enjoyed our new time together. We traveled on cruises and we even made one trip back to Poland and to Zychlin and Gostynin. This trip was not successful in that it brought back a flood of unpleasant memories of the Nazi occupation and of the ghettos. Every time our driver, who was familiar with the area, came close to old landmarks, I asked him to drive on and not stop.

There were exceptions like my old school where the principal took me around. As I stared at the empty desks I saw in my mind all of my old schoolmates. It was surreal. I summoned up the courage to visit our old rented home in Gostynin. I alighted the car and knocked on the door. And who should open it but our old landlord. After introducing myself his face turned into a smile and he embraced me and invited us in for some tea.

We talked for quite awhile and I told him about Israel and America and our children. This was probably the high point of my trip. Leaving the house, I was nearly overcome with emotion at being back in what was, before 1939, a place of peace and fond memories. It's sad that we cannot erase the bad times from our minds, but that is life. They say that 'you can never go back', but for some of us, 'we can never leave.'

Our next stop was the town of Chelmo and the concentration camp nearby. I felt that I needed to pay my respects to the thousands that were killed there. When I arrived at the site I said Kaddish for all the poor souls who suffered there. Out of the corner of my eye I saw a man and a woman appear from the nearby woods. I walked up to them and asked if there was something in the woods I should see and if they were Jewish. "No, we are not Jewish, but every year we walk this place and think about what people can do to people," they said.

He went on, "I am from Lodz, and when I was a little boy, my mother was taken into these woods. "Go in, you will see for yourself," he said. I thanked him and Rachel and I walked into the woods and came upon a huge grave site, so huge and imposing. I don't know what came over me but I broke down, filled with emotion. Finally, we traveled to Warsaw and the site of the ghetto that I first visited over seventy years ago. It, too, was a moving experience and served to reinforce in my mind that this would probably be the last time I would come back to Poland; it was too overwhelming.

Rachel and I returned to Florida and took up our lives, again. We were changed by the experience, but we have made happy and fulfilling lives for ourselves. We are surrounded by many people our age and with similar backgrounds and many that are different from us, but we spend each day in celebration of life and thank God with each sunrise that we have another chance to smile and laugh.

When a person laughs it's hard for the bad memories to break in. Maybe that is the secret of life. Do one thing at a time and make sure that the one thing you do brings joy to yourself and to others. What more is there?

During these many years since my liberation I have tried to explain to people in America what life was like for the Jews in Poland. I have been interviewed many times, but my greatest satisfaction comes from telling my story to groups of children. I am still doing this and probably will for as long as my memory and my breath hold out. It is important for a living person to stand before these impressionable souls and tell them that that part of man's history is something real and must never be allowed to happen again, anywhere.

I give them my words and my experiences and tell them that they have the power to change the world and that they must honor that power by not abusing it. So far, I have received so many letters from children that they fill a whole notebook. We Holocaust survivors have a special duty, as messengers. Though each of us will one day pass away, we must make sure that our stories live on and never fade into oblivion.

Even one small candle can light a room.

Some thoughts about survival

As I sit here in my home in Florida, I think back to my journey from teenager to adult, spending five years 'hiding in plain sight' after September 1, 1939. I ask myself the question that every Holocaust survivor asks himself or herself: "Why did I survive? Why me and not someone else?" If I go back to my early days, scrambling from farmhouse to farmhouse, fleeing the Nazis, and trying to fall asleep with my eyes open, I'm reminded of my grandfather who said, "When you dream about me, Yitzak, you will survive."

One night, my uncle and I were bedded down in a strange farmer's barn. We were both exhausted and had reached that point where, despite your fatigue, you have trouble falling asleep. We had been discussing the family a bit, speculating on what was going on in the ghetto. I should also say that my uncle didn't know my grandfather very well because he lived in Zychlin, so he couldn't contribute anything about him to our conversation.

Finally, we had reached the point where our bodies were ready for sleep and we both dozed off. Some hours must have passed, and my grandfather came to me in my sleep. He reassured me that I was alright and to relax, that I would survive.

Despite the peaceful nature of the message, I woke up, somewhat agitated because the dream was so real. I had to wake my uncle up. He was groggy, but listened to me, patiently. When I was done recounting the dream and describing how reassuring my grandfather was, my uncle simply said, "Go back to sleep." I couldn't blame him for not wanting to continue our conversation; dawn was soon breaking and we needed what rest we could get.

I knew, from that moment on, in my heart, that I would be alright. Granddad said so. If I ask myself, "Did God have a hand in keeping me alive all those years?," I cannot say for sure. I realize that to say such a thing makes me sound like a non-believer and somehow ungrateful, but such questions are difficult to answer with 100% certainty, despite your level of faith in God. I was a very good Jewish boy during the war.

I prayed regularly and observed our holy days and traditions, but I changed after the war. I asked a question of myself that many Jews and Gentiles asked, "How could a loving and caring God allow such atrocities to happen?"

I was always a curious child, not necessarily an overly-questioning one when it came to the physical world, but certainly curious when it came to things, spiritual. Where was God when he allowed my parents, brothers, uncles and friends to be killed by their captors? Was He standing in some corner of Heaven muttering to himself, "Well, I gave them all free will and they have chosen this path. They must accept the consequences and follow it to the end, without my interference?"

I always thought that there was certain sanctity in innocence. All one had to do was look at a newborn's face to know that. How could any new life be anything but holy? No, it will take wiser men than myself to answer the questions, "How and Why?" Perhaps it's not the wisdom of a man that qualifies him to answer it. Maybe it's a question that cannot be answered by anyone.

All I know is that many of my fellow survivors are plagued with it. My dear wife is one of them. Some have even written theological books about that simple question.

I believe in the Ten Commandments that God gave to Moses, and I believe that he who follows them will enrich his life and the lives of all who come in contact with him.

God inspires man and man inspires other men. That is how it is if you are a Rabbi, a Bishop or a simple teenage boy working on the railroad. The body needs food, but so does the mind and the spirit to survive. Hope gives the mind sustenance and faith nurtures the spirit. That faith that I speak of could also be the faith in one's self, inspired by God but fed by our own desire to survive. Faith was important to me, but so was living in the present, realizing my situation and the challenges that lay ahead AND making a plan to meet them.

I am convinced that my survival was in no small part due to my WILL to survive. While my loyalty was to my Jewish brothers and sisters and to be with them (like when I was with them in this giant hall waiting to be registered for the work camp), my head told me that to do that and die made no sense. This is why I escaped and why I ran from farmhouse to farmhouse and finally chose a life of subterfuge to stay alive.

Not every captive Jew could choose to run, nor could they hide their identity and get away with it; I knew I could, and that made the all-important difference for me. It was why I survived. I strongly object to the notion that "all the Jews had to do was resist and they would have lived." No one knows how threatening the barrel of a gun or an electrified fence or the noose of a rope can be until you are faced with it. It can sap the will to resist from even the hardiest of men. We must not forget that the Nazis understood human nature and how to manipulate their victims.

Their belief in themselves as the 'Master Race' gave them extra confidence and power, and it was but a small step from their knowledge of that power to the abuse of it. We were ordinary people, not soldiers. We had no weapons, no training in warfare or tactics. Yes, we had faith, but the more we expressed it, openly, the more brutal and repressive the punishment became. In the end, all that was left to the Jews was resignation to their fate.

The "Why?" question came up later when I was barbering at my shop in Newton. Vowing to get a theologian's answer, I contacted a local Rabbi. I asked him; "How was this, the Holocaust, possible? Could Rabbis from all over Poland and Germany and Hungary and wherever have not talked with one another and warned everybody and stopped it before it began to take hold?"

The Rabbi took off his glasses and looked at me a little sheepishly and said, "We couldn't. Sometimes it took months to a year for a letter to arrive." I couldn't believe the response. It sounded logical, but was unacceptable. Blaming it on the post office wasn't an answer to such a question, especially coming from a Rabbi. Seeing my dissatisfaction, he said, "Why not call a very renown Rabbi - a friend of mine in Boston - who happens to also be a professor? Ask him."

I asked if I could make a call, then and there, from the Rabbi's phone, and he said, "Yes." I dialed the number and got the Rabbi's assistant. "I am Isaac Kraicer, a Holocaust survivor. May I speak to Professor Solovyczch?" "I am sorry, but the professor is busy." I persisted and finally she relented. Rabbi Solovyczch came on the line. I asked him, "Rabbi, when I pray, let's say at Yom Kippur, the prayer for the suffering and the dying from the times of the Inquisition, why can you not put prayers in the book for victims of the Holocaust?"

He was coughing badly, and was obviously ailing, and my call didn't help him, I am sure, but he said, "You are right. You are right. Call me back, later. Six months went by. I again called the professor and asked if he had an answer for me. He said, "I am sorry young man. I am old and sick. I cannot do anything. I am sorry." I believed him. It is very often that even high-ranking men are powerless to make certain changes or to answer difficult questions.

Fortunately for all of us, some things do change over time. Today, in my synagogue, when we are saying the Kaddish, someone will be reciting the names of the Nazis' main concentration camps in memory of the victims.

Postscript

Rachel and I got married on October 28th of 1947. From that blessed union with a woman whose life I have shared for these past 70 years, we have three children. Jona (John), Zahava and Leonard, three grandchildren and two great grandchildren. Like so many survivors of the Shoah, my wife has suffered all of those years with the enormity of that sadness, often accompanied by depression. I am 92 years old as this being written. Mine is the story of but one thread in that vast and violent tapestry of history that allowed man's inhumanity to destroy the lives of millions whose only 'crime' was being different.

The Nazi years brought death, destruction and displacement to millions of people in many countries. It spread like wildfire, and the flames of that fire consumed everything in its path, leaving scars on everything it touched. Sometimes, in the dark of night, my mind wanders back to my village. I see Gostynin in the bright light and warmth of my childhood with my parents and grandparents, uncles, aunts and my two brothers all around me. We are all holding hands in a circle.

Then, the shadows start closing in, covering everything with blackness, turning my joy into sorrow as I remember how their lives ended, senselessly, prematurely, violently. My dreams alternate between that light and shadow, but with the passage of time have become more positive. I owe much to my family and to those millions of others who cannot dream or taste the warming rays of the sun. I must keep telling my story of the Holocaust so theirs can live alongside it. To me it is an unassailable moral obligation to do so. Such cruelty and human oppression cannot and must not be swept under the carpet of history or be allowed to reside in the shadows.

Such horrific events must visibly line our collective path to human recovery and the stories of those of us who have survived must be passed on from our generation to the next, lest the Holocaust be relegated to a mere footnote in history.

We survivors honor the departed by living life to the fullest... every day and in every way. To prevent this kind of tragedy from ever happening again, we must all love and cherish one another; celebrate our differences instead of fearing them; and we must never forget that the history of a people, any people, is written by the survivors and they have a sacred responsibility to get it right.

And if that means that we are destined to relive those moments for the rest of our lives, so be it. I saw the best and the worst of human beings during the occupation. I witnessed hatred and compassion, meaningless violence, vengeance, bigotry and forgiveness, grace and hospitality, friendship and sacrifice, loyalty and kindness. Human beings are not just one thing nor are they motivated by a single force. They are complex, often contradictory in their actions. They can pray on the Sabbath or at church on Sunday and turn abruptly into hypocrites on Monday. My faith in Hashem (God) has been tested many times during those horrible years. There were days when I cursed Him for deserting us and others when I asked for one simple sign of hope through an act of human kindness.

We wrestle with the eternal question of His existence and the meaning of life, itself, but when our survival is on the line we find the answer, and that answer is different for each of us.

I am truly blessed and I know it. These many years have taught me many lessons, but the most important of which is that faith and determination will ultimately decide our fate.

Today, I spend a fair amount of my time speaking to groups of schoolchildren about my experiences during the war. These fresh young faces have never known terror or been confronted by man's inhumanity to man. There have been occasions where I was hesitant to go into detail about the Nazi atrocities, but I was usually able to find the words to connect to the children.

After these encounters, I got dozens and dozens of letters of thanks from the children, and after reading them I know that I have done the right thing by making them aware of this chapter of history and the Holocaust and by cautioning them that this must never happen again. Here is a letter from one of the teachers.

Dear Isaac,

Thank you so much for coming to share your story with our students. I am truly in awe of your bravery and perseverance. Your years of that terrible time were filled with experiences that could be a movie! I am still shocked how many times you escaped and were never captured. God truly had a reason for you to survive the Holocaust, and I am honored to have met you. You have changed my life. I will pass on your story to my family and friends, as well as my future students, to make sure we never forget the Holocaust and its victims and survivors. I am truly sorry for your loss, but I am certain your family and loved ones are looking down on you with love and pride.

God bless you,
Danielle McConnell

A teacher's letter

School children at one of my talks

My beloved Rachel and I

My grown children Lenny, Zahava and John

In remembrance

I remember my mother's touch and my father's voice. I remember my brothers' playfulness. I remember the purity of prayer and the promise of spring on a cold winter's evening. I remember the dusty streets of my village and the verdant forest beyond. I remember the taste of cool water pumped from a deep well in our town square. I remember the yellow 'Jude' star and the 'P' patch. I remember the sound of a soccer ball hitting the net and the cheers of the crowd when it did. I remember all my friends and foes alike and what part they played in my life. I remember the constant fear of being discovered and the joy of liberation.

I remember reading of faraway places with exotic names and of celebrating Jewish holidays in the comfort of our home. I remember the first bite of food after having had none for days. I remember a gentle touch and a reassuring voice amid the chaos. I remember the weight of a freight car and the sound its giant wheels made when it was positioned among all the others. I remember the feeling of emptiness as I lay in a mound of hay, trying to sleep, wondering if that night was to be my last.

I remember the crack of an open hand as it hit my head and sent me reeling across a room as well as the kindness of a stranger who bravely hid me from harm. I remember the creaking hull of a transport ship that took me to a new land and the swerving gangplank that supported my feet as I left it. I remember the sweet taste of a Jaffa orange plucked from a tree and the fragrance of it when its skin was peeled away. There are hundreds more memories of living with hatred and with love, with suspicion and acceptance. While I will never forget my years spent in continual fear, I will not let it consume me or define me, either.

I know that my life is nearing its end, but I neither worry about it nor fear it. In my nine decades I have been spared much anguish and have experienced great joy. I have loved and been loved. I have extended my hand in friendship and have been rewarded for it. I have walked and run with the winds of change and have floated on the breeze of hope. I am ready for anything that may await me, but above all else, I am grateful for my life on this Earth.

Maps and Photographs

Map of Poland showing Gostynin and Zychlin
Map of concentration camps in Poland

My father Eliezer and mother Golda Rivka
Gostynin town square in 1939
The ghetto in Gostynin in 1939
Remnants of the Gostynin ghetto
SS executing Polish prisoners in Gostynin
The train station in Minden
Allied bombs took their toll on Minden
More destruction in Minden
Bombed out barracks in Minden
Good friends in Minden 1943
A musical break with friends in Minden 1944
The ghetto in Warsaw 1944
Bricha helped to smuggle Jews to Palestine
Me at Bricha's HQ in Hanover 1945
Bergen Belsen Concentration Camp 1945
Bergen Belsen barracks
Burning of Bergen Belsen barracks May 1945
Our Berlin Bricha gang 1946
My soccer team in Bergen Belsen 1946
Rachel and friends in kibbutz in Bergen Belsen 1946
On the kibbutz in Israel 1949
Rachel and Jona on the kibbutz 1949
Lenny and I at our home in Newton
Jona, Lenny and Zahava 1960
Rachel, Zahava and Lenny 1960
My barber shop in Newton
A teacher's letter
School children at one of my talks
My beloved bride and I
My grown children Lenny, Zahava and Jona (John)

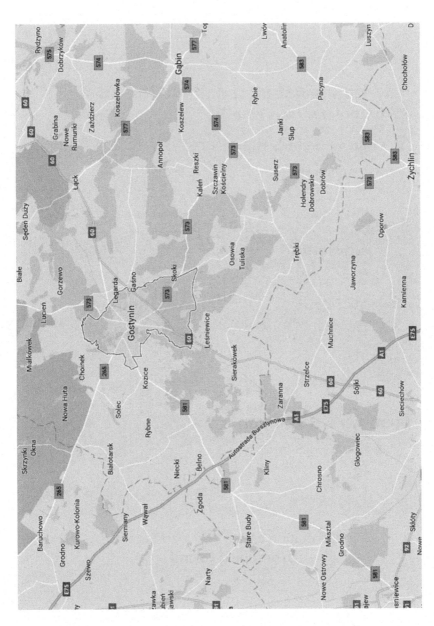

Map of Poland showing Gostynin and Zychlin

Concentration and extermination camps
in occupied Poland

My father Eliezer and mother Golda Rivka

Gostynin town square in 1939

The ghetto in Gostynin in 1939

Remnants of the Gostynin ghetto today

SS executing Polish prisoners in Gostynin

The train station in Minden

Allied bombs took their toll on Minden

More destruction in Minden

Bombed-out barracks in Minden

Good friends in Minden in 1943

A musical break with friends in Minden 1944

The ghetto in Warsaw

Bricha helped smuggle Jews to Palestine

Me at Bricha's Hanover HQ in 1945

Bergen Belsen concentration camp

Bergen Belsen barracks

Burning of barracks in Bergen Belsen in May 1945

Our Berlin Bricha gang in 1946

My soccer team in Bergen Belsen in 1946

Rachel and friends in kibbutz in Bergen Belsen 1946

On the kibbutz in 1949

Rachel and Jona in the kibbutz 1949

Lenny and I in Newton

John, Lenny and Zahava in 1960

Rachel, Zahava and Lenny in 1960

My barber shop in Newton, MA

Dear Isaac,

Thank you so much for coming to share your story with our students. I am truly in awe of your bravery and perseverance. Your years of that terrible time were filled with experiences that could be a movie! I am still shocked how many times you escaped and were never captured. God truly had a reason for you to survive the Holocaust, and I am honored to have met you. You have changed my life. I will pass on your story to my family and friends, as well as my future students, to make sure we never forget the Holocaust and its victims and survivors. I am truly sorry for your loss, but I am certain your family and loved ones are looking down on you with love and pride.

God bless you,
Danielle McConnell

A teacher's letter

School children at one of my talks

My beloved Rachel and I

My grown children Lenny, Zahava and John

Isaac Kraicer

The word 'survivor' is only part of the story of Isaac Kraicer's life. After being ripped from his boyhood home in his native Poland, he experienced the death of his entire family at the hands of the Nazi occupiers. Relying on his cunning and courage, he boldly defied the odds and thwarted numerous attempts at his capture while masquerading his true identity as a Jew. Working on the German railroad, he earned a reputation as an accomplished railroad man. After the war, he spirited hundreds of Jews out of Russia and Germany to Palestine. For his efforts, he was recognized by two Jewish organizations: the Bricha and the Haganah and rewarded with his own passage to the new Jewish state. Today, he lives with his wife, Rachel, in Florida, and devotes much of his time educating young people on the Holocaust.

Stephan Helgesen

A retired U.S. diplomat, Mr. Helgesen has written eight books and over 800 articles on politics, economics and social trends. Two of his books chronicle the lives of Holocaust survivors. He has lived and worked in over 30 countries, among them: Germany, The Netherlands and Denmark where he met many former members of the Danish and Dutch resistance and many survivors of the Shoah. He is currently the Honorary Consul for Germany in New Mexico and lives in the mountains outside Albuquerque.

Made in the USA
Columbia, SC
03 August 2018